CHARACTERIZATION AND TREATMENT OF TEXTILE WASTEWATER

CHARACTERIZATION AND TREATMENT OF TEXTILE WASTEWATER

BY

AAYLA LEE
HENRY MARSH

KNOWLEDGE BAKERS

ISBN: 9789390013449 (HB)

Published by : **Knowledge Bakers**
Pune, India
Email: knowledgebakers2019@gmail.com

Digitally Printed at : **Replika Press Pvt. Ltd.**

PREFACE

Textile wastewater is a type of industrial wastewater that is generated during textile manufacturing processes. This wastewater contains a range of pollutants, including organic compounds, dyes, heavy metals, and suspended solids, which can be harmful to the environment and human health if not properly treated. Characterization of textile wastewater is an essential step in developing effective treatment strategies. The characteristics of textile wastewater can vary depending on the type of textile manufacturing process used. Common pollutants found in textile wastewater include- Textile manufacturing processes involve the use of various chemicals, such as surfactants, bleaching agents, and finishing agents, which can lead to the presence of organic compounds in the wastewater. Textile wastewater often contains dyes, which can be difficult to remove and can cause environmental problems if discharged into water bodies. Textile wastewater may contain heavy metals such as lead, mercury, and chromium, which can be toxic to aquatic life and humans. Textile wastewater can contain a high level of suspended solids, which can cause clogging in treatment plants and affect the efficiency of the treatment process.

There are several treatment methods that can be used to treat textile wastewater, including physical, chemical, and biological methods. The choice of treatment method will depend on the specific characteristics of the wastewater and the desired quality of the treated water. Physical treatment methods involve the use of physical processes to remove pollutants from the wastewater. These methods include sedimentation, filtration, and adsorption. Chemical treatment methods involve the use of chemicals to remove pollutants from the wastewater. Common chemical treatment methods include coagulation-flocculation, oxidation, and advanced oxidation processes. Biological treatment methods involve the use of microorganisms to degrade organic compounds in the wastewater. These methods include activated sludge, anaerobic digestion, and bioreactors. Membrane technology is an advanced treatment method that uses membranes to filter pollutants from the wastewater. Membrane filtration methods include microfiltration, ultrafiltration, nanofiltration, and reverse osmosis. Wastewater is a major source of pollution that can have harmful effects on the environment and human health. Proper characterization of textile wastewater is essential in developing effective treatment strategies. A combination of physical, chemical, biological, and membrane treatment methods can be used to treat textile wastewater and achieve the desired quality of treated water. The implementation of efficient and sustainable treatment technologies will not only help in environmental conservation but also ensure a better quality of life for humans and aquatic life.

Provides an overview of the current state-of-the-art technologies for treating dye-containing wastewater in the textile industry. The technologies discussed include physical, chemical, and biological treatment methods, as well as advanced oxidation processes. Explains the characteristics of immobilized enzymes and discusses their potential applications in dye removal and also discusses the advantages and disadvantages of using immobilized enzymes and highlights the challenges associated with their use. Examines the effect of inorganic additives on the removal of textile dyes by ozonation and explains the mechanism of ozonation and discusses the role of inorganic additives in enhancing the efficiency of the process. Focuses on bioremediation and detoxification technologies for the treatment of dyes from textile effluent also highlights the challenges associated with bioremediation and discusses the potential for the technology to be scaled up for industrial applications. This book is intended for environmental persons like engineers, project managers, consultants, and water analysts everyone actively working on the environment, especially for researchers in textile wastewater.

We are grateful to all those persons as well as various books, manuals, periodicals, magazines, journals etc. that helped in the preparation of this book. In spite of the best efforts, it is possible that some errors may have occurred into the compilation and editing of the book. Further queries, constructive suggestions and criticisms for the improvement of the book are always welcomed and shall be thankfully acknowledged.

Aayla Lee
Henry Marsh

CONTENTS

Preface v

1. **A Review of State-of-the-Art Technologies in Dye Containing Wastewater Treatment – The Textile Industry Case** 1
   - » *Introduction*
   - » *Processes in textile industry*
   - » *Treatment processes of textile industry wastewaters*
   - » *State of the art processes*
   - » *Conclusions and recommendations*
   - » *References*
2. **Immobilized Enzymes – Characteristics and Potential Applications in Synthetic Dye Color Removal** 29
   - » *Introduction*
   - » *Enzyme Immobilization: Characteristics and applications*
   - » *Conclusion*
   - » *References*
3. **Effect of Inorganic Additives in the Textile Dyes Removal by Ozonation** 55
   - » *Introduction*
   - » *Dyeing wastewater treatment*
   - » *Materials and methods*
   - » *Results and discussion*
   - » *Conclusions*
   - » *References*

4. Bioremediation and Detoxification Technology for Treatment of Dye(s) from Textile Effluent **75**

» *Introduction*

» *Background to dye(s)*

» *The physical basis of color*

» *Classification of dye(s)*

» *The production and discharge of dye(s)*

» *The toxicity of dye(s)*

» *Pollution from the dye-containing effluents*

» *Dye removal techniques*

» *Conclusion*

» *References*

5. Heterogeneous Photocatalysis Remediation of Wastewater Polluted by Indigoid Dyes **93**

» *Introduction*

» *Heterogeneous photocatalysis degradation of Indigo carmine dye*

» *Conclusions*

» *References*

Index **115**

Chapter 1

A Review of State-of-the-Art Technologies in Dye-Containing Wastewater Treatment – The Textile Industry Case

Abstract

Recently, new single or hybrid/combined processes have attracted much attention for treatment of textile and dyeing wastewaters. These processes which may be termed as "state of the art technologies" are membrane separation processes, ultrasonic, photochemical and electrochemical processes. Although the conventional methods still have been tried with some new materials such as, new adsorbents or coagulants, employing the new generation methods such as, electrocagulation-electrooxidation, sonooxidation or photo oxidation are gaining in popularity when the treatment of textile wastewaters is discussed. The purpose of the book chapter is to bring an overview on the new treatment methods for textile wastewaters, one of the most important source of environmental pollution. Despite the fact that there is no uniform standard currently, many countries have legalized some strict discharging standards and scientists and researchers face new technologies including electrical, sonic, magnetic, optical and thermal methods. Although many researches on treatment of synthetic or real wastewaters with various methods are available, very few researches have been carried out on the cutting-edge technologies. Moreover, there are a lot of review article or book chapters on textile wastewater treatment processes individually based on each conventional process such as coagulation, adsorption, chemical oxidation, and biological decolorization. Therefore, in this part of the book, following major and minor titles are stated truly on the aforementioned new technologies. Besides, these parts are not only about cutting-edge technologies, but also related with conventional methods and their new applications in colored wastewater treatment area briefly.

Keywords: Textile wastewater treatment, decolorization, membrane processes, ultrasonic treatment processes, electrochemical treatment processes, photochemical treatment processes, hybrid processes

1. Introduction

Textile wastewaters are one of the most polluted wastewaters due to their characteristics, such as high chemical oxygen demand (COD) concentration, strong color, high pH and temperature, and low biodegradability [1–3]. These effluents can exhibit serious environmental problems and public health concerns if improperly disposed. These highly colored components, when discharged with wastewater into the water bodies, stop the reoxygenation capacity of the receiving water and cut-off sunlight, thereby upset biological activity in aquatic life [4]. Since diversity of textile products increases, different dyestuffs with highly varying chemical characteristics are used in this sector, which complicates further the treatment of textile wastewaters [1]. Several conventional methods have been applied for this purpose, such as adsorption, biological treatment, oxidation, coagulation, and flocculation [5–8]. Although these methods have been widely applied, they have some disadvantages. For example, adsorbents are usually difficult to regenerate [9]. Chemical coagulation causes extra pollution due to the undesired reactions in treated water and produces large amounts of sludge [3]. Biological methods are not suitable for most textile wastewaters due to the harmful effects of some commercial dyes on the organisms used in the process. Furthermore, these conventional methods are also usually expensive, and treatment efficiency is inadequate because of the large variability of the composition of textile wastewaters [10].

The main problem that environmental engineers have to deal with is the elimination of the wastewater's color, which is due to the remaining dyes. However, color removal has been a great challenge over the past decades, and up to now there is no single and economically attractive treatment that can effectively decolorize dyes, and new technologies for wastewater decolorization are especially needed [11–13]. Recently, new single or hybrid/combined processes have attracted much attention for the treatment of textile and dyeing wastewaters. These processes which may be termed as "state of the art technologies" are membrane separation, ultrasonic, photochemical, and electrochemical processes. Although the conventional methods still have been tried with some new materials such as new adsorbents or coagulants, employing the new generation methods such as electrocoagulation-electrooxidation, sono-oxidation, or photo-oxidation are gaining in popularity when the treatment of textile wastewaters is discussed.

The purpose of this chapter is to bring an overview on the new treatment methods for textile wastewaters, one of the most important sources of environmental pollution. Despite the fact that there is no uniform standard currently, many countries have legalized some strict discharging standards, and scientists and researchers face new technologies, including electrical, sonic, magnetic, optical, and thermal methods. Although many researches on treatment of synthetic or real wastewaters with various methods are available, very few researches have been carried out on the cutting-edge technologies. Moreover, there are a lot of review article or book chapters on textile wastewater treatment processes individually based on each conventional processes, such as coagulation, adsorption, chemical oxidation, and biological decolorization. Therefore, in this part of the book, the following major and minor titles are stated truly on the aforementioned new technologies. Besides, these parts are not only about cutting-edge technologies but also related to conventional methods and their new applications in colored wastewater treatment area briefly.

2. Processes in textile industry

2.1. General process description

The textile industry is a global industry in all around the world, which provides a huge income and employment for several countries. Besides, textile manufacturing includes several sequencing processes that are characterized as whole by consumption of resources, such as water, electricity, and fuel, and usage of several types of chemicals. Another important load of textile production on environment is the production of wastewater, which consists of many impurities such as dyes and pigments, heavy metals, and surfactants with high concentrations. These wastewaters should be treated before discharging into the surface water sources; otherwise, they can threaten the quality of water source and wildlife. It must not also be underestimated that a big amount of energy consumption is necessary for the treatment of wastewaters containing dye. After the treatment of wastewater, sludge remains, which includes high percentage of chemicals, and needs to be disposed with methods used for hazardous waste.

All these have totally enormous impact on environment, which makes it necessary to increase the efficiency and sustainability of processes to decrease the load on environment in long term. The content of dye of textile wastewater comes mainly from the dyeing and printing processes, including washing process; but before these processes, pretreatment steps should be applied for the quality of dyeing/printing. The process stages by textile industry can be summarized as follows:

- **Singeing:** The process of burning off protruding fibers from yarn or fabric.
- **Sizing:** The process of giving a protective coating on the warp yarn to minimize yarn breakage during the weaving.
- **Desizing:** The process of removing sizing agent from woven fabric prior to subsequent processes, such as bleaching, dyeing, and finishing.
- **Scouring:** The process of removing impurities.
- **Bleaching:** The process of removing or lightening colored materials.
- **Mercerization:** The process of improving lustre, dyeability, and strength of cellulosic material.
- **Dyeing:** The process of coloring fibers, yarns, or fabrics.
- **Printing:** The application of colorants in definite, repeated patterns to fabric, yarn, or sliver by any one of a number of methods other than dyeing.
- **Finishing:** The final process given to a textile material to give good appearance, functional properties, such as water-repellent, shrink-resistant, and wrinkle-resistant.

Washing and drying processes are also applied after different process stages, such as desizing, bleaching, and mercerizing, and especially after dyeing process to remove the dyestuff, which is not fixed on the textile [14–16].

2.2. Types and chemistry of dyestuffs

To color the final products of textile industry such as fabric, different dyestuffs are used after pretreatment steps of fabric. The textile dyes is an important part of not only the dyes but also the chemicals of the world business. The most used dyes in textile industry are on synthetic basis. They are produced mainly from coal tar and petroleum-based products. The dyes are sold in market as powders, granules, pastes, or liquid dispersions. The properties of textile materials such as fabric have been continually changed according to the new developments in textile industry. The dyes should also meet the demands of these new fabricated materials of textile industry. These can cause to increase the percent of the active materials in dyes, which causes more pollution in environmental systems. According to their chemical properties, the dyes can be classified as follows [17].

- Reactive dyes
- Acid dyes
- Basic dyes
- Disperse dyes
- Vat dyes
- Sulfur dyes
- Mordant dyes
- Direct dyes
- Ingrain dyes (Naphthol dyes)
- Solvent dyes (Lysochromes)
- Pigment dyes (Organic pigments)
- Other dye classes such as food dyes and natural dyes

Not 100% of the dyes are fixed to the fiber during the dyeing process. For example, reactive dyes show the minimum fixing range with 20–50% to cotton and viscose. A big part of the colored wastewater coming from textile dyeing processes is caused dyeing process such as cotton dyeing with reactive dyes with the poorest fixation property. Therefore, the fixation ratio of dye on textile product is also very important to minimize the dye consumption and production of colored wastewater from the industry [18].

2.3. Environmental effects of textile industry wastewaters

The most important load on environment caused by the textile industry can be summarized as follows:

- Consumption of natural and energy sources, such as water, fuel, and electricity.
- Usage of chemicals especially dyes by dyeing and printing processes.

- Production of wastewater with many impurities such as color, which has to be treated before discharging into the canalization or surface water [19].

During the treatment processes for the textile wastewater, a big amount of energy should be used and besides after the treatment process, sludge remains, which is evaluated as hazardous waste, and needs special disposal processes such as incineration which consumes also energy.

As seen, water consumption and pollution belong to the most important environmental issues regarding the textile industry. Therefore, the production organizations in textile sector should develop more efficient and environment friendly technologies to consume less water and to reduce discharged effluent increasing the quality of discharged wastewater at the same time to meet the discharge limitations [20].

During the production of textile products, big amounts of water are consumed especially by dyeing and printing processes. A textile facility with a daily production capacity of 8000 kg has a daily water consumption of nearly 1.6 million liters [21]. Nearly 25% of water of whole consumption is required for dyeing and printing processes. According to the US EPA [22], 40 liters of water is required averagely for dyeing 1 kg of cloth, changing according to the textile material and dyeing process. Water is also required for other processes such as washing of dyed textile material. Table 1 shows the consumption of water, chemicals, and energy for production of 1 kg of colored fabric.

System unit	Input	Conventional process
Pre-treatment	Water	20 l
	Solvent	120 kg
	Gas	—
	Energy	0.13 kwh
Dyeing	Water	20 l
	Solvent	20.98 g
	Dyestuff	10 g
	Auxiliary	25 g
	Energy	3.82 kwh
Washing	Water	10 l
	Washing agents	5 g
	Energy	0.16 kwh
Drying	Energy	0.04 kwh
	Gas	0.27 kwh

Table 1. Global inventory for the dyeing process (functional unit: 1 kg of colored fabric) [23]

There have been several efforts to decrease this enormous effect on environment caused by textile industry. Especially, the trends to decrease environmental load of textile products on environment at the design phase is a very important aspect, which affect the later stages of supply chain. Low impact dyes and processes managed by green technology, which require less water, is more effective than the efforts taken after production or during the production. Also the need for the more effective measurement of the textile processing systems is an important point. The processes should be traced and measured effectively to determine the load on environment of each used materials and processes [23].

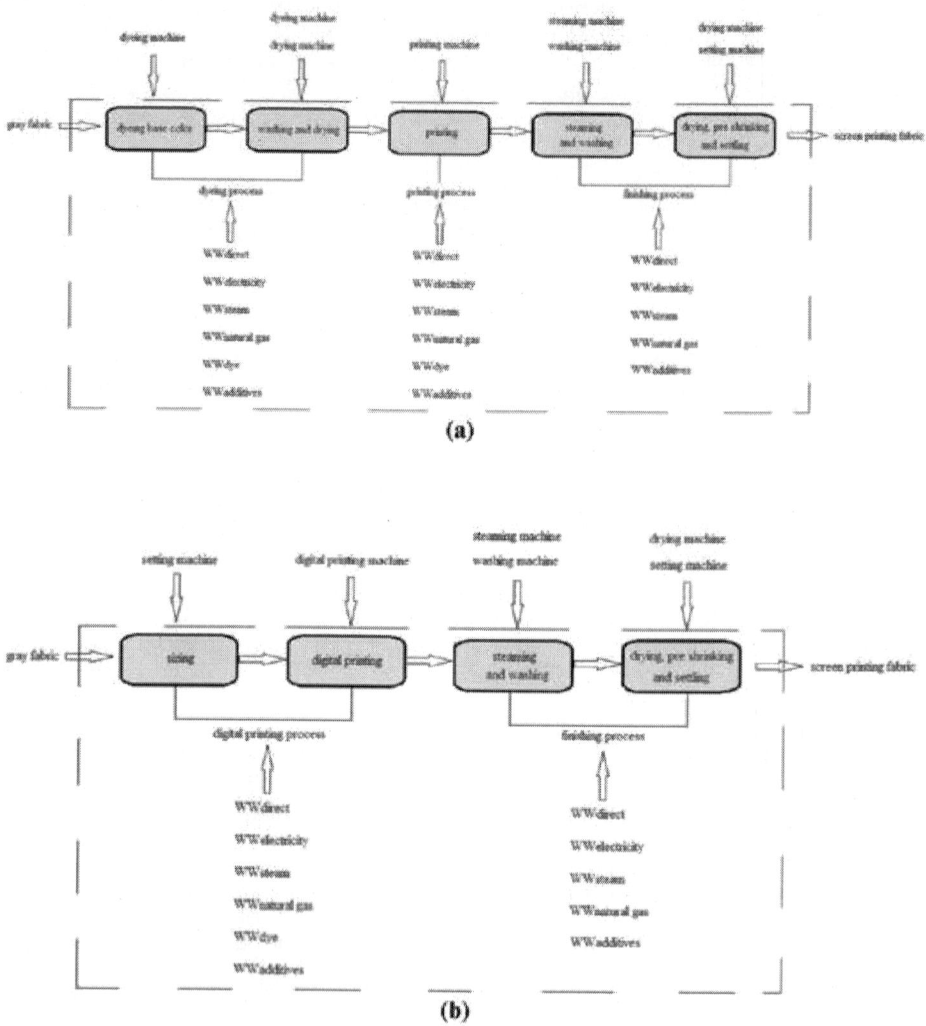

Figure 1. System boundary of the evaluation and production of screen printing (a) and digital printing (b) fabrics [20]. Water withdrawal (WW) is the volume of water taken from a catchment for production process.

Figure 1 is a good example to show the effect of using more technological processes to decrease the water consumption. The system boundaries of two production systems: one of which includes a screen printing and the other digital printing as printing process. The main water withdrawal is coming from both systems by the printing process. There is also indirect water withdrawal from other processes such as vapor production and water used for additives. It can be seen from Figure 3 also that digital printing system has a more compact system, which realizes the process without dissolving the dye in the water and reduces water use and pollution at the dyeing and printing processes. These kinds of technological developments by dyeing and printing processes are very important besides the increasing of the treatment efficiency and reuse of treated wastewater in textile industry [20].

In this context, new projects are supported by governmental and regional institutions. One of them is called BISCOL project co-founded by European commission. The aim of the project is to develop new technologies in dyeing processes, which make available to convert the raw material into the eco-viable final products. For this purpose, innovative technologies such as enzymatic synthesis of dyes or textile pre-treatment based on plasma technology have been used. The results which compare the environmental loads on environment of both conventional textile processes and processes supported by BISCOL project are shown in Figure 2. As shown in Figure 2, the BISCOL processes provide incredible benefits in terms of environmental pollution and consumption of natural resources [24].

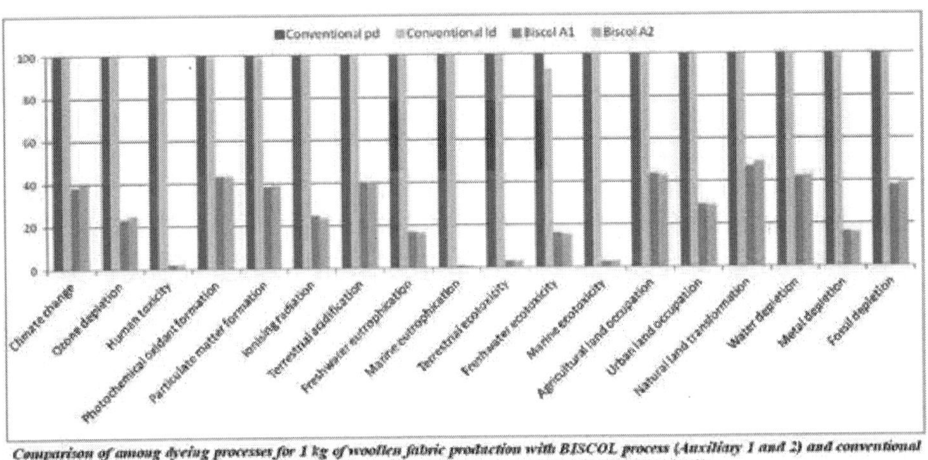

Figure 2. Comparison of dyeing processes for 1 kg woolen fabric production with BISCOL process (auxillary 1 and 2) and conventional ones (liquid and powder dye) [24].

2.4. Environmental standards for the discharging of textile industry effluents in the world

Typical textile wastewater characteristics in five different containers appearing in a study are shown in Table 2 [25]. Because of the strong characteristics of the textile wastewaters, there are strict limits for discharging of textile wastewater into the canalization or receiving environment in many countries. Textile facilities are not allowed to discharge their wastewater into aquatic environment or canalization requiring establishing wastewater treatment plants of which the outlet water has to meet the discharge limits according to receiving system. Also, polycyclic aromatic hydrocarbons (PAHs) are included in textile dyeing sludge as components of synthetic dyes, which are known to be potent carcinogens and given high priority for environmental pollution regulation and in risk assessment of industrial discharges [25, 26]. In Table 3, the discharge standards of water pollutants for dyeing and finishing of textile industry in a country are shown. The direct discharge limits show the limits to be obeyed when discharging directly into the aquatic environment. The indirect discharge limits show the limits to be obeyed when discharging into the canalization system. If the Tables 2 and 3 are considered together, it is seen that essential removal rate of pollutants in textile wastewater described by parameters such as COD, biological oxygen demand (BOD5), or TSS (total suspended solids) at least over 90% which makes necessary to establish well-designed wastewater treatment plants in the textile mills [27].

Parameters	C_1	C_2	C_3	C_4	C_5	C_6
pH	10.95	12.48	12.60	12.34	11.78	11.26
EC (mS/cm)	5.12	8.32	13.22	11.76	6.41	8.26
COD (mg/l)	3089	1916	1838	1463	2220	1871
BOD_5 (mg/l)	300	900	600	900	1375	1250
BOD/COD	0.1	0.47	0.33	0.62	0.62	0.67
TOC (mg/l)	898	686	563	614	439	629
TSS (g/l)	0.46	1.07	0.22	1.21	0.67	0.21
VSS (g/l)	0.26	0.61	0.12	0.71	0.01	0.11
		Ions (mg/l)				
Calcium (Ca)	6.94	1.34	9.33	10.88	11.9	7.64
Potassium (K)	1.13	8.13	68.84	90.84	110.8	17.13
Sodium (Na)	100.4	162.4	142.4	226.0	118.0	142.4
Magnesium (mg)	10.39	40.39	40.13	34.13	40.13	8.39
Heavy metals (mg/l)						
Copper (Cu)	0.003	0.001	—	0.011	—	—
Zinc (Zn)	0.092	0.018	0.106	0.104	0.179	0.012
Nickel (Ni)	—	—	0.027	—	—	—
Chrome (Cr)	—	—	—	—	—	—
Cadmium (Cd)	0.008	0.008	—	—	—	—
C: Container						

Table 2. Characteristics of real textile wastewater [28]

Parameters	Limit value (max)		Monitoring Location
	Direct discharge	Indirect discharge	
pH	6–9	6–9	Wastewater total outfall from factory
COD	100 mg/l	200mg/l	
BOD_5	25 mg/l	50mg/l	
TSS	60 mg/l	100 mg/l	
Color (dilution) ratio)	70	80	
Ammonia nitrogen	12 mg/l	20 mg/l	
N total	20 mg/l 35 mg/l (batik industry)	30 mg/l 50 mg/l (batik industry)	
P total	1.0 mg/l	1.5 mg/l	
Chlorine dioxide	0.5 mg/l	0.5 mg/l	
AOX	15 mg/l	15 mg/l	
Sulfide	1.0 mg/l	1.0 mg/l	
Anilines	1.0 mg/l	1.0 mg/l	
Antimony total	0.10 mg/l	0.10 mg/l	
Chromium VI	0.5 mg/l		wastewater outfall from factory workshop of production facility

Table 3. Discharge limits of typical contaminants for textile factory effluents [27]

3. Treatment processes of textile industry wastewaters

3.1. Conventional physochemical processes

The dyes could be used in higher amounts than needed actually for the dyeing or printing processes. As a result of insufficient bounding of dye molecules to the textile, unbounded dye molecules are released as the waste product. This causes 10% of dyes to be produced yearly out of the total usage as waste. The dyes have carcinogenic, mutagenic, allergic, and toxic nature on one hand, and on the other hand, they cause environmental pollution. High concentrations of BOD, COD, color, pH, and the presence of metals make the textile wastewater difficult to be treated. Because of these reasons, the combination of different treatment processes, such as conventional and/or advanced physical, chemical, and biological, is needed to be combined to treat these wastewaters [17]. Figure 3 shows the major pollutants discharged from various stages of a textile manufacturing industry.

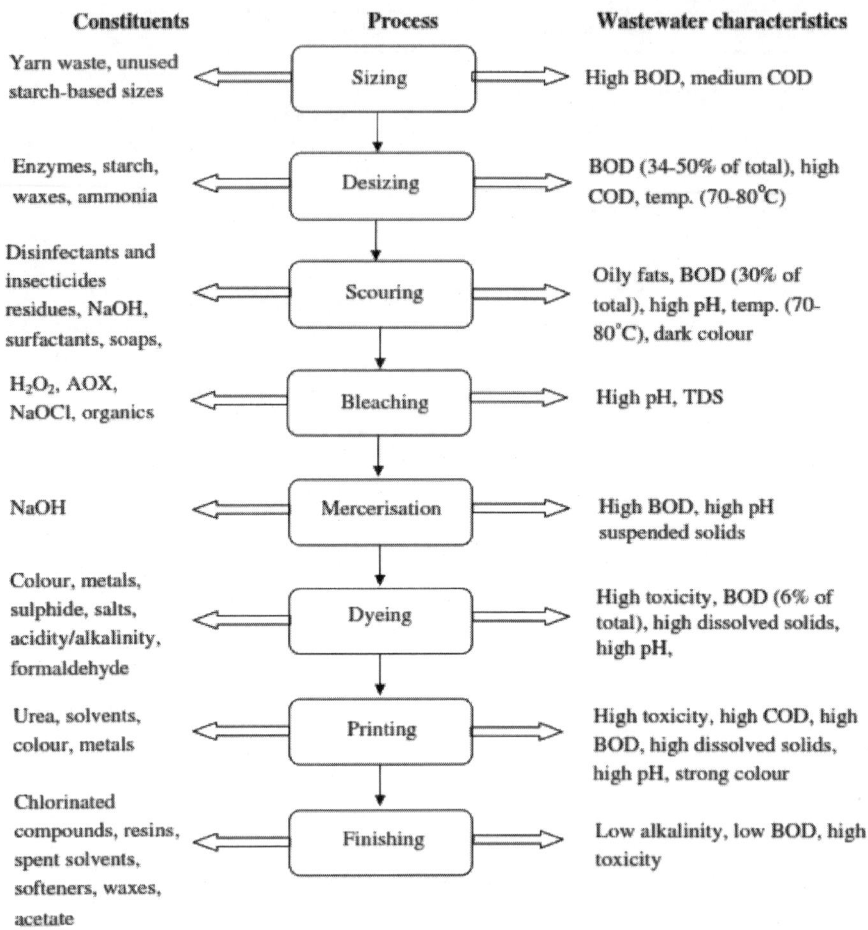

Figure 3. The component of major pollutants involved at various stages of a textile manufacturing industry [29].

By the treatment of industrial wastewater, mostly different physical, physicochemical, and biological treatment processes are used together depending on the pollutants to remove and discharge quality. These combinations are also used for textile wastewater, which constitutes an important part of the industrial wastewater.

The conventional physicochemical processes can be considered as follows:

- Coagulation/flocculation
- Adsorption
- Ion exchange

- Membrane separations
- Oxidation
- Cavitation [30].

According to the wastewater character and discharge limits, more than one process can be used together and also combined effectively with biological processes for the treatment of textile wastewater.

Coagulation and flocculation processes (C/F) are used in the treatment of industrial wastewater effectively. The aim of the process is to destabilize colloidal material using coagulants agents and after destabilizing to form aggregation of small particles with synthetic or natural polymers. Herewith, the bigger aggregates can be removed by separation processes like sedimentation easily [28]. C/F process is also used effectively by treatment of textile wastewater. Mostly, inorganic coagulants, such as aluminum sulfate ($Al_2(SO_4)_3$), aluminum chloride ($Al_2(Cl)_3$), and ferric sulfate ($Fe_2(SO_4)_3$), are used in the process. However, using inorganic coagulants has some disadvantages like high residual aluminum concentration, which can cause development of Alzheimer's disease and senile dementia [31].

Adsorption is one of the most efficient processes in the physical treatment of wastewater because of its efficient ability to separate dissolved/undissolved chemical compounds and easy operation [30]. The adsorption process is based on a surface phenomenon by which organic and inorganic pollutants are removed by adsorption on the surface of the adsorbent. The adsorbent materials like active carbon have a very large specific surface area, and if the absorbable solute comes into contact with the surface structure, they are concentrated on the solid surface because of the attraction forces between molecules. This process can be used effectively to remove the dissolved organic content of the textile wastewater [32].

The ion exchange process is also applied in the area of textile wastewater treatment effectively. Ion exchange is the reversible interchange of ions between a solid (ion exchange material) and a liquid in which there is no permanent change in the structure of the solid. In industrial wastewater treatment, the wastewater is the ion-containing solution from which the unwanted ions should be removed. Mostly, complex ion exchangers like ion exchange resins (functionalized porous or gel polymer) are used by industrial wastewater including textile wastewater for the ion source, which is to be exchanged with ions that are to be removed from aqueous matrix. Cation ion exchangers like weak acid cation exchange resins exchange the positively charged ions (cations), and the anion exchangers like weak base resins exchange negatively charged ions. In Figure 4, a cationic ion exchange resin is schematically shown by which the hydrogen ions are weakly bound to the negatively charged matrix. By the treatment of industrial wastewater, the hydrogen ions are given to the aqueous matrix and from the aqueous matrix; the unwanted ions like calcium (Ca^{2+}) are received and bound to the resin [33].

By textile wastewater treatment, the ion exchange process can be applied with the combination of other main processes, such as biological treatment or electrochemical techniques. After the biological treatment process, the residual dissolved organic carbon (DOM) consists of dissolved dye and auxiliaries, which are not biodegradable and can still exhibit acute and chronic

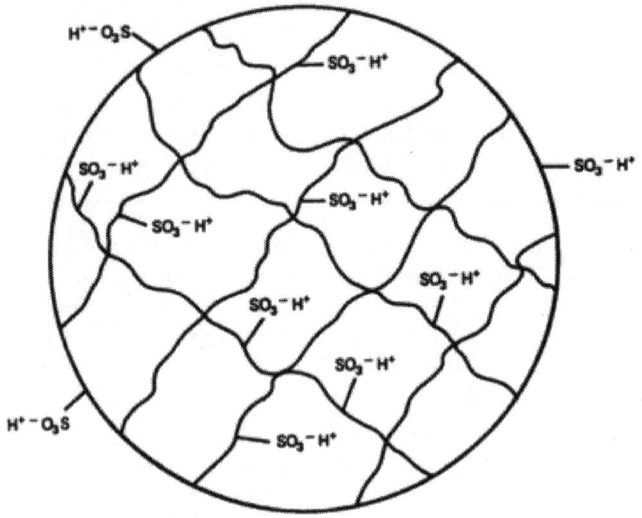

Figure 4. Cation exchange resin schematic showing negatively charged matrix and exchangeable positive ions [33].

toxicities. Dyes used by the textile industry are made up of chromophores and auxochromes, which are defined as typical anionic groups. Therefore, commercially available anion exchange resins can be employed in dye wastewater treatment for the removal of DOM [28]. However, ion exchange processes, which are mostly used by industrial wastewater treatments, are applied in fixed beds, which are expensive and exhibit flux restriction. Fan et al. investigated the removal of dissolved organic carbon after biological treatment process using magnetic anion exchange resin to find a more economical way to remove the nonbiodegradable DOM, which is toxic to aquatic environment. As a result, they found that magnetic anion exchange resin, which has remarkable regeneration behavior, could be used to remove DOM in actual biological treatment process effluent of textile wastewater [34–36].

3.2. Biological processes

Almost all kinds of commercial and industrial wastewaters have biological degradable constituents. Although the textile wastewater is a strong polluted industrial wastewater, an important part of the organic content is the biodegradable (See the Table 2). Therefore, the aerobic, anoxic, and anaerobic biological processes and their combinations have been applied effectively by the treatment of textile wastewaters. Except the biological degradation, the processes of adsorption and complexation with microorganism play an important role by treatment processes for the removal of pollutants like heavy metals [37].

Textile wastewaters contain many refractory compounds, which are biologically hard or nondegradable and mostly toxic for environmental systems. The biodegradation can also occur for these compounds that have organic structure, but in comparison with easy biodegradable organics, they can need slow processes like anaerobic digestion and specific microorganisms [37].

Biological treatment systems can be divided into different categories such as aerobic, anaerobic, and anoxic systems or according to growth system of microorganism suspended growth and attached growth. Figure 5 shows the biological treatment methods, which are applied also for the treatment of industrial wastewaters including textile wastewater.

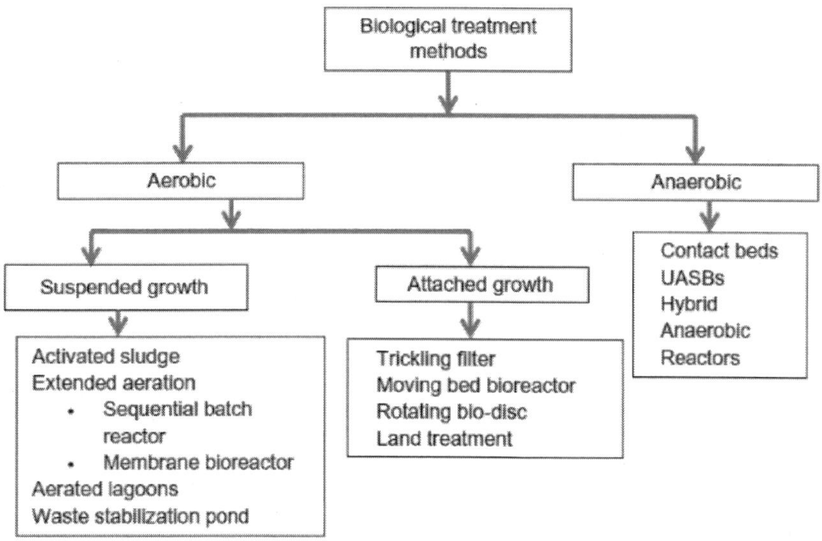

Figure 5. Biological wastewater treatment methods [38].

The systems are categorized according to the existence of the air in the treatment system. In the aerobic systems, oxygen is present in biological systems as the electron acceptor. On the other hand, oxygen is absent in the anaerobic system and the electron acceptor is the organic material. Figure 6 shows the principles of two biological treatment processes. The oxygen is used as oxidation element of organic material and carbon dioxide, water, and new cells are produced as final products in aerobic system. However, no air (thus molecular free oxygen) should be absence in the anaerobic medium and methane, carbon dioxide and new cells is produced at the end of the digestion process.

Recently, both aerobic and anaerobic processes have been applied for the treatments of textile wastewater successfully. According to the physicochemical and oxidation methods, the biological treatment methods of textile wastewater have significant advantages. They are firstly more environmental friendly because no chemical usage is needed mostly and the produced sludge as the result of the cell production has a low chemical content and amounts.

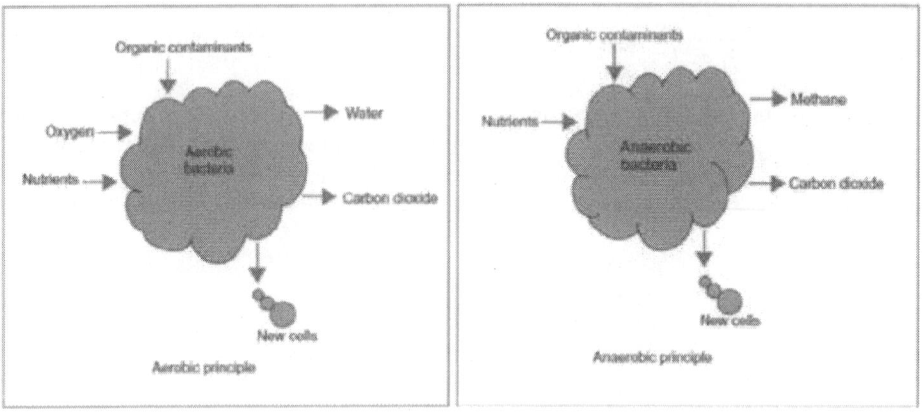

(a) (b)

Figure 6. Aerobic (a) and anaerobic (b) degradation principles [38].

They are more cost-competitive because of the less or no usage of chemicals. The yielding end products are nontoxic or have complete mineralization, and they require less water consumption compared to physicochemical methods [39, 40].

Conventionally, the biological treatment of textile wastewater occurs under anaerobic, facultative anaerobic, and aerobic conditions by different groups of bacteria. By the treatment process, pure cultures of microorganism or composed of mixed microbial populations can be used. The mixed microbial cultures can be more effective because of their synergistic metabolic activities compared with the pure cultures by the treatment process of textile wastewater [41]. The dye molecules can be attacked by different individual strains at different positions of bonds and the co-existing strains may help for the further decomposition processes. This is very important for the total mineralization of organic content of textile wastewater, because by not complete degradation of organic content, toxic organic compounds can be present in the discharge water already [42].

The membrane processes are also used effectively with combination of biological processes by the treatment of the industrial wastewaters. The system is called as membrane bioreactor and has many advantages compared with the conventional biological system using final sedimentation tank. By the biological treatment systems, the microorganisms consume the organic matter and as a result new cells are produced. The exceeded sludge that contains the old microorganisms should be removed from the system for the stability of the system. This separation process of sludge from mixed liquor can be achieved mainly in two ways. The conventional system, which has been used at many treatment plants, is the sedimentation process. By the sedimentation process, the sludge flocks are precipitated in the sedimentation tanks and removed from the bottom of the tank. Sometimes chemicals like flocculants can be used to accelerate the sedimentation process. Recently, membrane separation processes have been applied effectively as an alternative separation process to the conventional sedimentation. By the membrane process, the separation of sludge from the mixed liquor occurs with the help of a membrane with a significant pore wide. The biological membrane processes have many advantages compared to the sedimentation processes like high quality of discharge water, high sludge age, less excess sludge production, less area need, and more effective biological degradation. Because of these advantages, membrane bioreactors are also used effectively by the treatment of textile wastewaters.

4. State of the art processes

4.1. Membrane processes

Membrane process is the transport of substances between two fractions with the help of membranes, which are permeable or nonpermeable for specific substances to be removed from the matrix or to be concentrated. For different separation purposes, different membrane processes are applied, which are classified according to membrane art, size of the particles to separate, and separation mechanism. Table 4 gives an overview about the membranes operated under pressure. The transitions between the single membrane processes are flexible [43].

Membrane process	Pore width [nm]	Pressure interval ΔP [bar]	Permeability [L/ m².h.bar]	Membrane type	Application
Microfiltration	50–5000	0.1–2	>50	Porous membrane	Separation of suspended solids
Ultrafiltration	2–200	1–5	10-50	Porous membrane	Concentration, fractioning and treatment of macromolecules in fluid systems
Nanofiltration	1–2	5–20	1,4-12	Nonporous membrane	Fractioning of dissolved materials in fluid systems
Reverse osmosis		10–100	0,05-1,4	Solution-diffusion membrane	Concentration of dissolved materials in fluid systems

Table 4. Under pressure operated membranes [43]

The membranes are applied by the treatment of textile wastewater as a separated process or in combination of other processes especially with biological processes. The membrane bioreactors are the combination of the membrane and biological processes and have a very wide application area in industrial wastewater treatment. The separated application of membranes for the treatment of textile wastewater has also been applied effectively for this purpose. The main advantage of membrane processes compared with the chemical treatment of textile wastewater is no usage of the chemicals. On the other hand, membrane processes also have disadvantages, mainly fouling. Fouling occurs in time during the operation with the clogging of the pores of the membranes, which results in the decrease of the flux and increase of the head loss. The quality of the discharge water from the membranes also decreases therefore the total performance of membrane process decreases because of the fouling [44].

Imer investigated the treatment performance of the polysulfone (PS) ultrafiltration membranes by the treatment of textile wastewater. The membranes were produced with phase inversion method under different temperatures. By the study, real textile wastewater is used with the following properties—conductivity: 5370 μS/cm, COD: 3094 mg/l, color: 1.47 (abs @530 nm), pH: 9.0, and suspended solids: 33 mg/l. The phase inversion production was conducted under four different temperatures from 25 to 65°C. The highest removal efficiency was achieved with the membrane produced under 65°C with 99% COD and 99% color removal [45].

In another study, hollow fiber nanofiltration membranes were investigated for the treatment of textile wastewater at laboratory and pilot scale. The operation was conducted under different conditions, such as temperature, conductivity of textile wastewater, and pH values. As a result, the recovery potential of the salts included in the textile wastewater was determined for the reuse of the salts at the next stage of the dyeing process. Because the textile wastewaters have high salt concentration, salt accumulation of the membranes in the membrane (internal concentration polarization) and on the membrane surface (external concentration polarization) can decline the flux. This can be prevented with the periodical washing of the membrane with the antiscaling solution The rejection of dye was over 98% in the study, which indicates that the membrane technologies are not only a treatment process but also a method to recover the dye and salt from textile wastewater [46].

4.2. MBR processes

Membrane bioreactor (MBR) is the combination of a membrane process (like ultrafiltration or microfiltration) with a suspended growth bioreactor. The MBR processes have significant advantages compared to the conventional biological treatment systems. High quality of discharge water, less production of exceeded sludge, and high concentration of mixed liquid suspended solids are the main advantages of MBRs. Except these, they need smaller area than the conventional systems because the membranes can be operated and installed in the biological reactor. The nitrogen and phosphorus removal also occurs at higher efficiency in MBRs. By two steps, membrane configuration nanofiltration or reverse osmosis steps can be used to meet the discharge limits or salt removal from the outlet of the MBR system. The recently conducted studies show that the membrane techniques can also exhibit high performances by the treatment of textile wastewater in the meaning of the high quality of discharge water and reuse possibilities of the auxiliary chemicals used for dyeing process.

In the study of Yurtsever et al., aerobic and anaerobic bioreactors were compared with regard to treatment efficiency of textile wastewater including azo dyes. No important change by the effluent concentration of azo dyes was observed with increasing azo dye concentration by the influent. This can be explained with the cleavage of the azo dye at low redox potentials [47].

Friha et al. investigated the treatment efficiency of the aerobic submerged MBR using textile wastewater as influent. In the system, a flat sheet membrane module was used with operating transmembrane pressure (TMP) ranging between 70 and 350 mbar. The system was operated during 6 months, and stable treatment results were gained at the end of the operation. Except the high removal efficiency for pollution parameter color, COD, BOD_5, and SS (color, 100%; COD, 98%; biochemical oxygen demand (BOD_5), 96%; suspended solids (SS), 100%), an important decrease by toxicity of wastewater was achieved, which indicates that the membrane processes can be operated effectively by the treatment of textile wastewater [28].

4.3. Ultrasonic oxidation processes

The energy given by the ultrasonic source to the wastewater results in the cavitation, which is the nucleation and behavior of the bubbles in the wastewater. Cavitation is the formation of cavities which also grow and collapse with each other. Cavities provide the condition of strong oxidizing to occur by way of production of hydroxyl radicals and also hydrogen peroxide. In the wastewater treatment, the cavitation bubbles act as a microreactor in which the volatile organic compounds are oxidized [47, 48]. The reaction chain of consisting of radicals through the ultrasonic cavitation is shown as follows [44]:

ultrasound

$$H_2O \rightarrow H^{\cdot} + HO^{\cdot} \tag{1}$$

ultrasound

$$O_2 \rightarrow 2O \tag{2}$$

$$H^{\cdot} + O_2 \rightarrow HOO^{\cdot} \tag{3}$$

$$O + H_2O \rightarrow 2HO^{\cdot} \tag{4}$$

The ultrasonic catalysis (sonocatalysis) processes are among the advanced oxidation processes, which are also applied with combination of the other advanced oxidation processes like photo catalysis. The process is based on the production of radical molecules like hydroxyl radicals ($HO^{\cdot}$) with the help of an energy source. This source can be acoustic, photolytic, or hydrodynamic energy for the treatment of textile wastewater. The sonocatalysis reactions can be applied in combination with other source such as photolytic energy. This can increase the interaction between radical and dye molecules and therefore the efficiency of the treatment of the textile wastewaters [48].

4.4. Photochemical oxidation processes

The photochemical oxidation processes are also among the advanced oxidation processes, which are applied effectively as alternative method to the conventional processes. The photochemical oxidation processes are also based on the production of highly reactive radical, such as hydroxyl radicals, which can degrade the recalcitrant organic materials included in the textile wastewater. The use of photochemical oxidation processes can be applied under solar radiation, which enhances the production of hydroxyl radicals ($OH^{\cdot}$) and provides to realize the treatment processes at lower costs [49, 50].

4.5. Electrochemical processes

Electrocoagulation also offers an alternative method for the removal of color by textile wastewater to the chemical coagulation by which metal salts or polymers and polyelectrolytes are used to break the stable emulsions and suspensions. By electrocoagulation, metal plates such as iron or aluminum are used as electrodes to produce highly charged polymeric metal hydroxide species continuously in the water. These ions with opposite charges destabilize the colloids, allowing them to coagulate [19]. Because no chemical is applied during the process, electrochemical processes have been used advantageous as an alternative technology to chemical coagulation for treatment of industrial wastewaters particularly textile and dyeing wastewaters [51–56]. Electrochemical process can also be used for the production of ferrous iron and/or hydrogen peroxide, thereby allowing the generation of hydroxyl radicals. This process is a similar process with electrocoagulation. The difference between two processes is adding of H_2O_2 with in various concentrations before the electrolysis [57, 58].

In a most recent study, four different iron-based processes were applied for the decolorization of textile wastewater; electrocoagulation, electrochemical fenton, electro-fenton, and peroxi-coagulation for decolorization of real textile wastewater. The fenton process is an important process to degrade the refractory chemicals through chemical oxidation by hydroxyl radicals (OH). The important point of the Fenton process is the production of ferrous iron and/or hydrogen peroxide for the oxidation of organic materials and other refractory chemicals. At pH value of 3, they achieved decolorization efficiency by 94.4 %, which indicates the better oxidation performance of produced hydroxyl radicals at low pH values. The removal efficiency of color increase by biodegradability and energy consumption for four processes were compared. In the study, the most important parameters that affect electrocoagulation efficiency are determined as pH value and the electrical current. The highest removal efficiency for color was achieved at the pH value of 6.5 and by an electrical current of 300 Ma. They also determined the optimum electrical current for both the highest energy efficiency and removal efficiency as 200 Ma [52]. In the study, the biodegradability of textile wastewaters was also investigated after iron-based electrochemical treatment processes. The biodegradability is an important parameter for industrial wastewater pointing out how the organic content of discharged wastewater can be degraded by the microorganisms in aquatic environment. The ratio of BOD_5/COD is the main parameter to determine the biodegradability of wastewater. If the ratio is high, it shows that the biodegradable part of the organic matrix is high and the organic constituents in the discharged wastewater can be eliminated more easily at aquatic environment. Figure 7 shows that all iron-based electrochemical treatment methods provide an increase by biodegradability of raw textile wastewater. The highest increase was seen by Fenton process supported by electrochemical methods, because hydroxyl radicals (OH·) can oxidize the resistant organic material to smaller ones, which can be degraded by microorganisms easier [57].

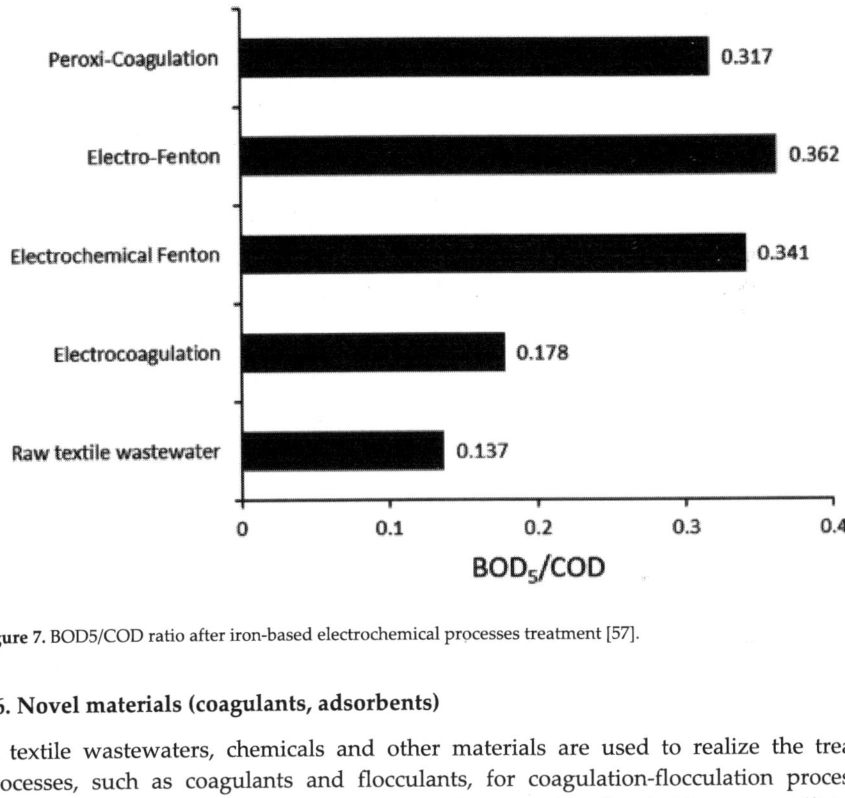

Figure 7. BOD5/COD ratio after iron-based electrochemical processes treatment [57].

4.6. Novel materials (coagulants, adsorbents)

In textile wastewaters, chemicals and other materials are used to realize the treatment processes, such as coagulants and flocculants, for coagulation-flocculation process and adsorbents for adsorption process. New materials are continually tried for a more efficient and cost-effective processes to develop.

By the coagulation process, mainly the chemical materials such as aluminum sulfate ($Al_2(SO_4)_3$), aluminum chloride ($Al_2(Cl)_3$), and ferric sulfate ($Fe_2(SO_4)_3$) are used. New coagulant agents, such as natural coagulants, have been used successfully by C/F process using the treatment of textile wastewater instead of inorganic coagulants. Natural coagulants have many advantages over chemical agents by treatment textile wastewater like particularly biodegradability, low toxicity, low residual sludge production, and low cost [31]. Renault et al. [59] also reported that using natural polymers reduces the required inorganic coagulant dosage, which results to produce less sludge, because more compact flakes by C/F process are produced. In the study of Freitas et al., okra mucilage is used (*abelmoschus esculentus*) as natural coagulant aid dissolved in distillated water and their efficiency was compared to chloride ferric (chemical agent) in C/F process of textile wastewater treatment. They determined an important increase by the removal of pollution parameters, such as color, COD, and turbidity. The amount of Fe^{3+} was also decreased up to 72.5% using a small amount of okra mucilage [31].

Activated carbon is used for the treatment of textile wastewater, but this process is very expensive; therefore, the cost analysis should be done carefully before the establishment of the process [60]. There are also cheaper products, which have been recently used by the adsorption process. Hydroxyapatites ($Ca_5(PO_4)_3(OH)$) belong to these materials, which are abundant in the nature, and can be applied effectively by the treatment of textile wastewater. Lemlikchi et al. investigated the adsorption kinetic of textile dyes on synthetic hydroxyapatite in aqueous solution. After adsorption process, during the adsorption process, the precipitation is also applied for the separation of hydroxyapatite saturated with pollutants in the wastewater. The co-precipitation was carried out at pH = 8 at batch mode, and settling time for the three textile dyes Hydron Blue (HB), Solophenyl Blue (SB), and Solophenyl Turquoise (ST) was almost 1 day. After settling, the supernatant was filtered and analyzed by UV-vis. By scanning electron microscope (SEM) analysis, it was seen that HAP grains are strongly bonded for the HB and for the SB. Lemlikchi et al. explained this adsorption process with the strong interaction between phenol, sulfonate, and amine groups in the dyes molecule and calcium ions. This study shows that the textile wastewater can be treated effectively with adsorbent material different from active carbon with lower costs [60].

4.7. Hybrid processes

Because the textile wastewaters contain many pollutants including hard or nonbiodegradable compounds, hybrid systems can be applied more effectively to use the advantages of each process. The physical, chemical, and biological process has advantages and disadvantages. For example, the chemical usage and production of sludge with high chemical content are the most important disadvantages of the coagulation-flocculation process. On the other hand, some nonbiodegradable compounds included in the textile wastewater can be precipitated and removed wastewater by C/F process. Therefore, the most efficient and cost-effective system combination has to be investigated according to the structure of the wastewater to be treated.

In the study of Sun et al., the removal of organic compounds and nitrogen in an anaerobic–anoxic–aerobic membrane bioreactor process (A^2O-MBR) for the treatment of textile wastewater was investigated. The two different membranes were used and submerged in the aerobic reactor symmetrically to observe the biofouling behavior of two membranes observed through the TMP. One of them was hollow fiber membrane made of polyvinylidene fluoride (PVDF) with a nominal pore size of 0.1 μm, and the other one was flat-sheet membrane. As a result, the organic matters and nitrogen were removed from the textile wastewater efficiently. For many organic matters, high removal ratios were achieved. On the other hand, very low removal efficiencies were seen for some hard biodegradable organic matters such as styrene with 2%. Also, combinations of acids and oxidizing agents were offered as a good solution for chemical washing to minimize the biofouling. The schematic diagram of the pilot-scale AO-MBR system was showed in Figure 8.

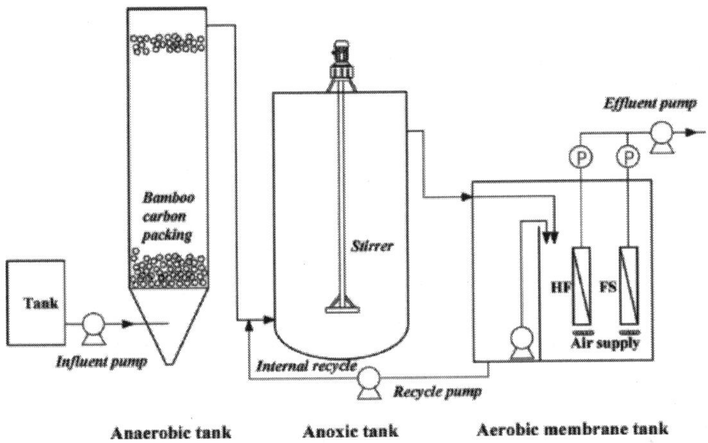

Figure 8. Schematic diagram of the pilot-scale AO-MBR system [61].

Some specific hard biodegradable pollutants can be degraded with the help of advanced oxidation processes [62]. Lee et al. [62] investigated the elimination of 1,4-dioxane contained in the textile wastewater by membrane photoreactor. UV lamps was used as photon source and TiO_2 was used as catalyst.As a result, they determined that the depredation in bioreactor with the support of photocatalytic reactions can satisfy the drinking water guidelines. The dosage concentration of TiO_2 should have been applied in high levels because of the low adsorption of 1,4-dioxane onto TiO_2 particles. The chemical precipitation methods can be applied before the biological processes to enhance the BOD_5/COD ratio. Figure 9 shows the schematic diagram of a treatment plant for textile wastewater located in Jiangmen of Guangdong Province-China.

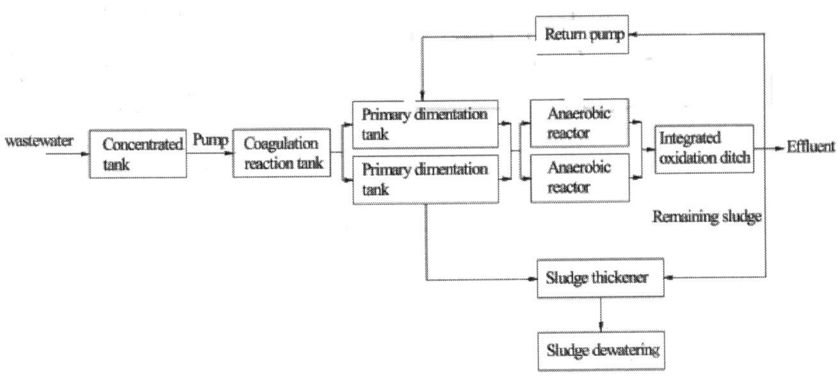

Figure 9. Schematic diagram of a textile wastewater treatment plant located in China [63].

The textile wastewater has the properties of high alkaline, color and organic matter content, and low biodegradability with 0.25 BOD_5/COD ratio. To increase the BOD_5/COD ratio before the biological processes, coagulation with $FeSO_4$ and following precipitation is applied. After chemical treatment, the two staged anaerobic-aerobic biological treatment processes are applied. The discharge limits are met according to local regulations.

The biological treatment is not sufficient for the removal and degradation of recalcitrant compounds in textile wastewaters. Therefore, chemical oxidation methods are applied before or after the biological processes for increasing biodegradability of wastewater or degradation of nonbiodegradable compounds. Punzi et al. [64] investigated the degradation of recalcitrant compounds and the removal of toxicity of textile wastewater by applying ozonation after anaerobic treatment. In that study, 99% of the color and 85–90% of COD were removed from a synthetic textile wastewater containing 100–1000 mg/l of the azo dye.

5. Conclusions and recommendations

The purpose of the book chapter is to bring an overview on the new treatment methods for textile wastewaters, one of the most important sources of environmental pollution. Despite the fact that there is no uniform standard currently, many countries have legalized some strict discharging standards, and scientists and researchers face new technologies including electrical, sonic, magnetic, optical, and thermal methods. Although many researches on treatment of synthetic or real wastewaters with various methods are available, very few researches have been carried out on the cutting-edge technologies. Moreover, there are a lot of review article or book chapters on textile wastewater treatment processes individually based on each conventional processes, such as coagulation, adsorption, chemical oxidation, and biological decolorization. Therefore, in this part of the book, following major and minor titles are stated truly on the aforementioned new technologies.

Textile effluents are highly polluted wastewaters with high concentration of chemical and biochemical oxygen demand, suspended and colloidal solids, salts, heavy metals, and other hard or nonbiodegradable organic matters, which is an important threat for environment when discharge criteria are not carefully considered. These wastewaters have complex structure and large emissions, which make them very hard to handle. Because mostly only one treatment process could not be sufficient to remove the pollutants effectively, the biological, physical, and chemical processes are used separately or in one process to support each other in a combined treatment plant. Among these processes, for example, membrane systems are very effective separation systems to be applied in the treatment of various impurities from textile wastewater. Membrane bioreactors have higher investment and operational costs compared with conventional biological processes, but they have very high quality of discharge water and reuse chances of valuable materials included in textile wastewater are high.

The adsorption process is also an important process, which can be combined with membrane processes like nanofiltration. But the adsorption materials such as active carbons are expensive materials; therefore, cheaper materials like different natural polymers are preferred. Electrooxidation or sonophotocatalysis process can be applied before the biological process to cleavage the bounds of the dye compounds and make them biodegradable. If the wastewater is desired to be used in the process again, an ion exchange process could be needed at the end of the process. As seen, the process combination can differ according to the structure of textile wastewater and discharge purposes. But it must not be forgotten that the green technology methods by the production of dye are more efficient and cost-effective methods to prevent the pollution and increase the reuse chances of materials contained in wastewater. Therefore, the use of natural eco-friendly materials has been investigated recently widely in the world, which is degraded in the biological treatment systems and environment more easily.

References

[1] O'neill FR, Hawkes DL, Lourenco ND, Pinheiro HM, Delee W. Colour in textile effluents-sources, measurement, discharge consents and simulation: a review. Chem. Technol. Biotechnol. 1999;74:1009-1018.

[2] Pela A, Tokat E. Color removal from cotton textile industry wastewater in an activated sludge system with various additives. Water Res. 2002;36:2920-2925.

[3] Gao BY, Wang Y, Yue QY, Wei JC, Li Q. Color removal from simulated dye water and actual textile wastewater using a composite coagulant prepared by polyferric chloride and polydimethyldiallylammonium chloride. Sep. Purif. Technol. 2007;54:157-163.

[4] Nassar MM, Magdy YH, Removal of different basic dyes from aqueous solutions by adsorption on palm-fruit bunch particles Chem. Eng. J. 1997;66:223-226.

[5] L. Szpyrkowicz C, Juzzolino SN, Kaul A. Comparative study on oxidation of disperse dyes by electrochemical process, ozone, hypochlorite and fenton reagent. Water Res. 2001;35:2129-2136.

[6] Harrelkas F, Azizi A, Yaacoubi A, Benhammou A, Pons MN. Treatment of textile dye effluents using coagulation-flocculation coupled with membrane processes or adsorption on powdered activated carbon. Desalination. 2009;235:330-339.

[7] Lu X, Liu L, Yang B, Chen J. Reuse of printing and dyeing wastewater in processes assessed by pilot-scale test using combined biological process and sub-filter technology. J. Clean. Prod. 2009;17:111-114.

[8] Ghorbani M, Eisazadeh H. Removal of COD, color, anions and heavy metals from cotton textile wastewater by using polyaniline and polypyrrole nanocomposites coated on rice husk ash. Compos. B Eng. 2013;45:1-7.

[9] Daneshvar N, Sorkhabi HA, Kasiri MB, Decolorization of dye solution containing Acid Red 14 by electrocoagulation with a comparative investigation of different electrode connections. J. Hazard. Mater. 2004;B112;55-62.

[10] Vlyssides AG, Loizidou M, Karlis PK, Zorpas AA, Papaioannou D. Electrochemical oxidation of a textile dye wastewater using a Pt/Ti electrode. J. Hazard. Mater. 1999;70:41-52.

[11] Georgiou D, Aivasidis A, Hatiras J, Gimouhopoulos K. Treatment of cotton textile wastewater using lime and ferrous sulfate. Water Res. 2003;37:2248-2250.

[12] dos Santos AB, Cervantes FJ, Van Lier JB. Review paper on current technologies for decolourisation of textile wastewaters: perspectives for anaerobic biotechnology. Bioresour. Technol. 2007;98:2369-2385.

[13] Ghanbari F, Moradi M. A comparative study of electrocoagulation, electrochemical Fenton, electro-Fenton and peroxi-coagulation for decolorization of real textile wastewater: Electrical energy consumption and biodegradability improvement, J. Environ. Chem. Eng. 2015;3:499-506.

[14] Tyrone LV. Textile Processing and Properties: Preparation, Dyeing, Finishing and Performance, Amsterdam-The Netherlands, Elsevier;1994. ISBN: 978-0-444-88224-0.

[15] Parisi, ML, Fatarella E, Spinelli D, Pogni R, Basosi R. Environmental impact assessment of an eco-efficient production for coloured textiles, J. Clean. Prod. 2015;108:51-524.

[16] Tortora PG, Merkel RS. Fairchild's Dictionary of Textiles 7th edition, New York-USA, Bloomsbury Publishing Inc., 2009. ISBN: 9780870057076

[17] El-Nemr A, editor. Non-Conventional Textile Waste Water Treatment. In series: Pollution Science, Technology and Abatement, New York-USA,Nova Publishers; 2012. 279 pp.

[18] Mughal MJ, Saeed R, Naeem M, Ahmed AM, Yasmien A, Siddiqui Q, Iqbal M. Dye fixation and decolourization of vinyl sulphone reactive dyes by using dicyanidiamide fixer in the presence of ferric chloride. J. Saudi Chem. Soc. 2013;17:23–28.

[19] Alkaya E, Demirer GN. Sustainable textile production: a case study from a woven fabric manufacturing mill in Turkey, J. Clean. Prod. 2014;65:595-603.

[20] Chen L, Ding X, Wu X. Water Management Tool of Industrial Products: A case study of screen-printing fabric and digital printing fabric. Ecol. Indic. 2015;58:86–94.

[21] Kant R. Textile dyeing industry an environmental hazard. Nat. Sci. 2012;4:22-26.

[22] US EPA. Best Management Practices for Pollution Prevention in the Textile Industry, 1996.

[23] Parisi, ML, Fatarella E, Spinelli D, Pogni R, Basosi R. Environmental impact assessment of an eco-efficient production for coloured textiles, J. Clean. Prod. 2015;108:51-524.

[24] Bioprocessing for Sustainable production of COLoured textiles [Internet]. 2016. Available from: http://www.biscol.unisi.it [Accessed: 2016-02-05].

[25] Li H. The study on cleaner production index system for oil & natural gas exploitation (thick oil). Environ. Prot. Oil Gas Fields 1. 2003;16–18.

[26] Xun-An Ning,, Mei-Qing Lin, Ling-Zhi Shen, Jian-Hao Zhang, Jing-Yu Wang, Yu-Jie Wang, Zuo-Yi Yang, Jing-Yong Liu, Levels, composition profiles and risk assessment of polycyclic aromatic hydrocarbons (PAHs) in sludge from ten textile dyeing plants. Environ. Res. 2014;132:112–118.

[27] China – Discharge Standards of Water Pollutants for Dyeing and Finishing Of Textile Industry [Internet]. 2016. Available from:http://www.sgs.com/en/Our-Company/News-and-Media-Center/News-and-Press-Releases/2015/07/SafeGuardS-12115-China-Discharge-Standards-of-Water-Pollutants-for-Dyeing-and-Finishing-of-Textile.aspx [Accessed: 2016-02-06].

[28] Friha I, Bradai M, Johnson D, Hilal N, Loukil S, Ben Amor F, Feki F, Han J, Isoda H, Sayadi S. Treatment of textile wastewater by submerged membrane bioreactor: In vitro bioassays for the assessment of stress response elicited by raw and reclaimed wastewater. J. Environ. Manag. 2015;160:184-192.

[29] Cumnan S. The Use of Constructed Wetland For Treating Azo Dye From Textile Wastewater [thesis]. Suranaree University of Technology; 2011.

[30] Hung YT, Wang LK, Shammas NK. World Handbook of Environment and Waste Management: Air and Water Pollution Control, Toh Tuc Link-Singapore, World Scientific Publishing Co. Pte. Ltd. 2012; ISBN: 978-981-4327-69-5.

[31] Freitas TKFS, Oliveira VM, de Souza MTF, Geraldino HCL, Almeida VC, Fávaro SL, Garcia JC. Optimization of coagulation-flocculation process for treatment of industrial textile wastewater using okra (A. esculentus) mucilage as natural coagulant. Ind. Crops Prod. 2015;76:538–544.

[32] Rashed MN, Adsorption Technique for the Removal of Organic Pollutants from Water and Wastewater. In: Rashed MN, editor. Organic Pollutants - Monitoring, Risk and Treatment, Rijeka-Croatia, InTech; 2013. 229 pp.

[33] DOWEX Ion Exchange Resins, Fundamentals of Ion Exchange [Internet]. 2016. Available from: http://msdssearch.dow.com/PublishedLiteratureDOWCOM/dh_0032/0901b803800326ca.pdf?filepath=liquidseps/pdfs/noreg/177-01837.pdf&fromPage=GetDoc [Accessed: 2016-02-07].

[34] Fan J, Li H, Li CSW, Li A. Dissolved organic matter removal using magnetic anion exchange resin treatment on biological effluent of textile dyeing wastewater. J. Environ. Sci. 2014;26:1567–1574.

[35] Shuang CD, Li PH, Li AM, Zhou Q, Zhang MC, Zhou Y. Quaternized magnetic microspheres for the efficient removal of reactive dyes. Water Res. 2012;46:4417–4426.

[36] Raghu S., Basha AC. Chemical or electrochemical techniques, followed by ion exchange, for recycle of textile dye wastewater. J. Hazard. Mater. 2007;149: 324–330.

[37] Tchobanoglous G., Burton LF., Stensel HD. Metcalf and Eddy Wastewater Engineering: Treatment and Reuse. 4th ed., New York-USA, McGraw-Hill. 2003.

[38] Ranade V, Bhandari V. Industrial Wastewater Treatment, Recycling and Reuse, 1st ed., Oxford-UK,Butterworth-Heinemann; 2014. 576 pp.

[39] Banat IM, Nigam P, Singh D, Marchant R. Microbial Decolorization of Textile-Dye-Containting Effluents: A Review. Bioresour. Technol. 1996;58:217-22.

[40] Rai H, Bhattacharya M, Singh J, Bansal TK, Vats P, Banerje UC. Removal of dyes from the effluent of textile and dyestuff manufacturing industry: A review of emerging techniques with reference to biological treatment. Crit. Rev. Environ. Sci. Technol. 2005;35: 219-238.

[41] Chen BY, Chang JS. Assessment upon species evolution of mixed consortia for azo dye decolorization. J. Chin. Inst. Chem. Eng. 2007;38:259-266.

[42] Forgacs E, Cserhati T, Oros G. Removal of synthetic dyes from wastewaters: A review. Environ. Int. 2004;30:953-971.

[43] Kraume M. Transport Processes and Apparative Applications in Process Technic, Heidelberg-German, Springer-Verlag,,; 2002 (In German)

[44] Amini M, Arami M, Mahmoodi NM, Akbari A. Dye removal from colored textile wastewater using acrylic grafted nanomembrane. Desalination. 2011;267:107–113.

[45] Koseoglu-Imer YD. The determination of performances of polysulfone (PS) ultrafiltration membranes fabricated at different evaporation temperatures for the pretreatment of textile wastewater. Desalination. 2013;316:110–119.

[46] Ong YK, Li FY, Sun SP, Zhao BW, Liang CZ, Chung TS. Nanofiltration hollow fiber membranes for textile wastewater treatment: Lab-scale and pilot-scale studies. Chem. Eng. Sci. 2014;114:51–57.

[47] Yurtsever A, Sahinkaya E, Aktas Ö, Uçar D, Çınar Ö, Wang Z. Performances of anaerobic and aerobic membrane treatment of synthetic textile wastewater. Biores. Technol. 2015;192:564–573.

[48] Reddy RD, Dinesh KG, Anandan S, Sivasankar T: Sonophotocatalytic treatment of Naphthol Blue Black dye and real Textile wastewater using synthesized Fe doped TiO. Chem. Eng. Process. 2016;99:10–18.

[49] Spuhler D, Rengifo-Herrera J, Pulgarin C. The effect of Fe^{2+}, Fe^{3+}, H_2O_2 and the photo-Fenton reagent at near neutral pH on the solar disinfection (SODIS) at low temperatures of water containing Escherichia coli K12. Appl. Catal. B. 2010;96:126–141.

[50] Oller I, Malato S, Sánchez-Pérez JA. Combination of advanced oxidation processes and biological treatments for wastewater decontamination – a review. Sci. Total Environ. 2011;409: 4141–4166.

[51] Ventura A., Jacquet G, Bermond A, Camel V. Electrochemical generation of the Fenton's reagent: application to atrazine degradation. Water Res. 2002;36:3517–3522

[52] Eyvaz M. Treatment of textile wastewaters by using electrocoagulation with different electrode connections Fe and Al. MSc Thesis, in Turkish. 2006; Kocaeli, Turkey.

[53] Bayramoglu M, Eyvaz M, Kobya M: Treatment of the textile wastewater by electrocoagulation: economic evaluation Chem. Eng. J. 2007;128: 155–161.

[54] Kobya M, Bayramoglu M, Eyvaz M. Techno-economical evaluation of electrocoagulation for the textile wastewater using different electrode connections. J. Hazard. Mater. 2007;148:311-318.

[55] Eyvaz M, Kirlaroglu M, Aktas TS, Yuksel E. The effects of alternating current electrocoagulation on dye removal from aqueous solutions. Chem. Eng. J. 2009;153:16-22.

[56] Yuksel E, Gurbulak E, Eyvaz M. Decolorization of a reactive dye solution and treatment of a textile wastewater by electrocoagulation and chemical coagulation: Techno —economic comparison. Environ. Prog. Sustain. Energy. 2012;31(4):524-535.

[57] Ghanbari F, Moradi M. A comparative study of electrocoagulation, electrochemical Fenton,electro-Fenton and peroxi-coagulation for decolorization of real textile wastewater: Electrical energy consumption and biodegradability improvement. J. Environ. Chem. Eng. 2015;3:499–506

[58] Ventura A, Jacquet G., Bermond A., Camel V.: Electrochemical generation of the Fenton's reagent: application to atrazine degradation. Water Res. 2002;36:3517–3522.

[59] Renault F, Sancey B, Badot PM, Crini G. Chitosan for coagulation/flocculation processes: An eco-friendly approach. Eur. Polym. J. 2009; 45: 1337–1348.

[60] Lemlikchi W, Drouiche N, Belaicha N, Oubagha N, Baaziz B, Mecherri MO. Kinetic study of the adsorption of textile dyes on synthetic hydroxy apatite in aqueous solution. J. Ind. Eng. Chem.. 2015;32:233–237.

[61] Sun F, Suna B, Hua J, Hea Y, Wu W. Organics and nitrogen removal from textile auxiliaries wastewater with A_2O-MBR in a pilot-scale. J. Hazard. Mater. 2015;286:416–424.

[62] Lee KC, Beak HY, Choo KH. Membrane photoreactor treatment of 1,4-dioxane-containing textile wastewater effluent: Performance, modeling, and fouling control. Water Res. 2015;86:58-65.

[63] Wang Z, Xue M, Huang K, Liu Z. Textile Dyeing Wastewater Treatment. In: Hauser P, editor. Advances in Treating Textile Effluent, Rijeka-Croatia, InTech; 2011. 154 pp.

[64] Punzi M, Nilsson F, Anbalagan A, Svensson BM, Jönsson K, Mattiasson B, Jonstrup M: Combined anaerobic–ozonation process for treatment of textile wastewater: Removal of acute toxicity and mutagenicity. J. Hazard. Mater. 2015;92:52–60.

Chapter 2

Immobilized Enzymes – Characteristics and Potential Applications in Synthetic Dye Color Removal

Abstract

In recent times, enzymatic approaches have been used in treatment of colored wastewater/industrial effluents. Peroxidases are very useful in removal of recalcitrant toxic compounds or transforming them into innocuous products. Although much attention has been paid in the utilization of biocatalysts in several fields, their involvement in solving the environmental problems has gained support. Enzymes in soluble states have limitations of catalytic ability and stability. As the complexity of the effluents increases, the ability of the enzymes to execute its catalytic potential decreases. Therefore, one of the approaches to improve stability, catalytic ability, reusability and shelf life of enzymes is by immobilization. Work in the area of enzyme technology has provided significant clues that facilitate using enzymes optimally at large scale by cross-linking, entrapping and immobilizing. The current article presents an insight into the use of peroxidases immobilized on several different supports for the dye color removal of synthetic dyes as well as several different contaminants.

Keywords: Peroxidases, Immobilization, Dye decolorization, Continuous reactor

1. Introduction

Technological innovations have contributed immensely in wastewater treatment especially with respect to removal of synthetic dye color. Enzymatic approaches have immense potential and consequently have gained much attention in recent times. These biomolecules are not only ecofriendly but exhibit specificity in targeting and reducing hazardous wastes. Peroxidases (EC 1.11.1.7) are a key to wastewater treatment and distributed in a variety of plants, animals and microorganisms. These are heme-containing enzymes with specificity towards a wide spectrum of substrates. Essentially, these enzymes require hydrogen peroxide to act on a variety of aromatic compounds. The enzyme in its presence is oxidized to a catalytically active form which subsequently reacts with phenolic contaminants. During their course of action they get inactivated which is due to the formation of free radicals which are adsorbed on the enzymes catalytic site and blocks the binding of the substrate molecules.

Peroxidases are very useful in removal of recalcitrant toxic compounds or transforming them into innocuous products [1, 2]. The characteristic of a given waste upon treatment with peroxidases is sufficiently changed so that it is more amenable to subsequent treatments. Being enzymes, they have higher reaction rates, milder operating conditions (relatively low temperature and in the entire aqueous phase pH range) greater stereo-specificity, and consequently in comparison to chemical catalysts are selective and efficient. Although, biocatalysts have been exploited in several areas, their use in dealing with environmental problems is the need of the time. Soluble form of enzymes has inherent limitations of stability and the complexity of effluents make them vulnerable to denaturation and consequently loss of catalytic potential. To a certain extent these limitations can be overcome by immobilizing these enzymes on suitable supports which would improve their catalytic parameters.

Peroxidases in conjunction with hydrogen peroxide have been extensively used in removal of aromatic compounds present in effluent discharge. Enzymatic treatment of wastewater has certain merits over conventional strategies. While there is simplicity in controlling the enzymatic processes, they can be exploited in a wide range of pH, temperature, salinity, contaminant concentration, recalcitrant materials. Nevertheless, the effective use of these enzymes was limited due to their non-reusability, high purification cost and sensitivity to the denaturants in wastewater. In order to overcome some of these constraints immobilization of these enzymes on various supports opens up new avenues for exhaustive utilization. With the advancement of technology, enzymes can be immobilized optimally at large scale on several different supports by cross-linking and entrapping. The current article provides an insight of using simple supports to immobilize peroxidases and testing it for dye color removal of synthetic dyes

2. Enzyme Immobilization: Characteristics and applications

2.1. Immobilization of polyphenol oxidase on Celite 545

Achieving immobilization of enzymes by simple adsorption has a practical advantage of regeneration of support and consequently easy replacement of deactivated enzymes with a fresh batch of active catalysts [3]. An insoluble support is not only inexpensive but the relatively simple adsorption techniques make the approach interesting. Polyphenol oxidases (PPO) finds application in the analytical determination of cyanide, azide, aromatic amines, phenols and catechols such as neurotransmitter substances and related metabolites [4-6]. PPO have been immobilized on various supports and used for the treatment of wastewater [7]. Although, several techniques based on the PPO treatment have been developed for the remediation of industrial wastewater but the cost of the processes has limited its use [8, 9].

Celite is an inexpensive diatomite carrier with properties desirable for the immobilization of enzymes. It has been used as a support even while using partially purified protein preparations [10]. Celite exhibits preferential selectivity for tyrosinase and other blue proteins indicating that this material is useful for isolating copper containing proteins [11]. PPOs from potato were immobilized on Celite 545 [12]. The adsorption of PPO on Celite 545 was significantly affected by varying the pH of the buffer [13]. Maximum binding was recorded at pH 7.0 whereas above and below this pH, the binding decreased. For instance upon altering the pH to 5.0, the bound enzyme activity was only 68% as compared to the maximum at pH 7.0. Similar variation has also been documented for immobilization of PPO on various other matrices [14]. While studying the influence of pH on soluble and Celite-PPO, immobilized preparation exhibited wider pH-activity profile with no difference in pH-optima between pH 5.0 and pH 6.0. Also, immobilized PPO retained significantly higher fraction of enzyme activity in the acidic range [15]. Celite bound PPO from brinjal shows higher pH-optima as compared to potato PPO [7].

Temperature activity profile is an important parameter to assess the functional suitability of the enzyme which may be subjected to varying thermal conditions. Celite - PPO retained greater fraction of the catalytic activity at higher temperatures. A complete loss in activity was noticed at 80°C with soluble PPO fractions whereas the immobilized counterpart retained 27% of the original PPO activity [7]. Similar alteration in temperature optima was reported for fig tree latex ficin immobilized on Celite [15]. The retention of biological activity in thermal denaturation studies suggested that Celite bound preparation was significantly more stable as compared to soluble counterpart. Celite bound potato PPO has better stability as compared to the Celite bound brinjal PPO [7].

As compared to soluble counterparts, immobilized states of enzymes were superior in stability towards denaturants. Immobilized enzymes exhibited an enhancement in catalytic activity as against soluble states which were able to exhibit half of its initial activity after an incubation of 2 h. Treatment with 4.0 M urea for 2 h under similar conditions did not cause much loss in catalytic potential. Effluent discharge is also loaded with several detergents. It was observed that soluble form of peroxidases in 1.0% SDS for 1 h lost 61% of its original activity, the immobilized counterparts retained over 83% of initial activity under similar experimental conditions. Potato PPO on incubation with increasing concentration of Triton X 100 and Tween 20 (0.2 – 1.0%, v/v) underwent catalytic stimulation. Immobilized preparations of PPO were more activated as compared to soluble states of enzymes. Findings are suggestive of existence of potato PPO in its partially active form, which was fully activated in presence of lower concentrations of various detergents [16, 17]. The activation of immobilized potato PPO activity by the presence of some pure detergents suggested that this behavior is significantly fruitful for using such preparations for the treatment of organic pollutants even in the presence of such type of detergents.

The behavior of soluble and immobilized enzyme preparations upon exposure to various water-miscible organic solvents like (dimethylformide) DMF, dioxane, n-propanol and acetonitrile suggested that the immobilized enzyme preparation exhibited retention of very high enzyme activity even when the strength of the organic solvent was very high whereas the soluble enzyme preparation lost its activity rapidly when exposed to water-miscible organic solvents. The immobilized enzymes exhibited over 38% of its initial activity as compared to soluble form which could retain only about 24% activity under identical exposure to 60% dimethylformide. In the presence of 60% n-propanol immobilized enzymes showed enhanced activity whereas soluble form underwent a decrease in activity, manifesting only 75% of its initial activity. An exposure of these two states of enzymes to 60% (v/v) acetonitrile suggested better performance of immobilized preparation expressing 40% in comparison to soluble forms with only 19% of the original activity. The activity of Celite bound PPO and free form enzymes underwent stimulation in enzymatic activity at concentrations of organic solvent up to 30% (v/v). In case of immobilized PPO, the stimulation was more pronounced. Several investigators have shown the immobilization of potato PPO via adsorption on chitin, chitosan, and Eudragit S-100, etc. supports resulted in the stabilization of PPO activity against water-miscible organic solvents [3, 18].

2.2. Immobilization of bitter gourd (*Momordica charantia*) peroxidase on DEAE cellulose

An anion exchanger, diethyl aminoethyl (DEAE) cellulose has been used to immobilize the salt fractionated and dialyzed bitter gourd proteins (BGP) [19]. DEAE-BGP preparation was compared with its soluble counterpart for its stability against pH, heat, urea, detergents, water-miscible organic solvents and proteolytic enzyme (trypsin). BGP was immobilized in very high yield on DEAE cellulose and it bound 590 units of BGP/g of the ion exchanger. The preparation was highly active and exhibited very high effectiveness factor. Effectiveness factor of an immobilized enzyme is a measure of internal diffusion and reflects the efficiency of the immobilization procedure. In this case, the yield of immobilization was quite superior over other methods used for the immobilization of peroxidases [20, 21]. BGP was tightly associated with DEAE cellulose as treatment with 0.5 M NaCl did not resulted in any significant detachment of enzyme molecules. This matrix bound BGP exhibited high degree of stabilization against pH, thermal and denaturation with urea. These findings suggested the use of DEAE cellulose as matrix for high yield and stabilization of enzymes and proteins that have also been supported by other workers [22, 23]. The immobilized BGP preparation exhibited broadening in pH–activity profiles as was the case with Con A-Sephadex bound BGP. DEAE cellulose and Con A-Sephadex bound BGP was remarkably stable against trypsin mediated proteolysis [24]. DEAE cellulose bound BGP was quite resistant against denaturation induced by detergents. The native conformation of enzymes is unaffected in the presence of lower concentration of detergents. Lower concentration of detergents improves the catalytic activity of enzymes more so in immobilized states which also exhibit remarkable stability against higher concentrations of detergents [4].

The structure of enzymes can be affected by the presence of organic solvents and several aromatic compounds present as pollutants. Therefore, it is essential to assess the stability of enzymes against such solvents. BGP immobilized on DEAE matrix are stable on exposure to dioxane, DMSO and propanol. Immobilization involving multipoint confers protection against organic solvents in co-solvent mixtures [25, 26]. Several workers have shown that potato polyphenol oxidase adsorbed on chitin exhibited variation in their properties as compared to free form in aqueous-organic co-solvent mixtures. They have also dwell on polyphenol oxidase, peroxidase, trypsin and acid phosphatase and showed that within a specific concentration range of water-miscible organic solvent in the medium the activity of enzymes are stimulated [3]. It has also been shown that enzymes immobilized on protein supports were also quite resistant to denaturation induced by various water-miscible organic solvents [27, 28].

BGP preparation has enhanced stability against pH, heat, urea, proteolysis, detergents and water-miscible organic solvents when immobilized on DEAE matrix. This aspect of improved stability to various form of denaturing conditions upon immobilization has been described elsewhere [22, 29, 30]. The resistance to protease is an additional attribute to the adsorption of BGP on anion exchanger. Looking at the convenience of immobilization and retention of catalytic activity, DEAE bound BGP may open up new avenues in treatment of organic pollutants in effluents from industrial units. As only non-covalent interactions hold the BGP to DEAE cellulose, desorption of enzyme from support cannot be ruled out. Additionally, these enzymes could cross-linked by bi-functional or multifunctional reagents to prevent the leakage of peroxidases from matrix.

2.3. Immobilization of turnip (*Brassica rapa*) peroxidase on bioaffinity support

Polysaccharides could be used for bioaffinity based purification of Con A from the extract of jack bean. Bioaffinity based media can be prepared for immobilizing enzymes obtained from crude preparations. Turnip peroxidase (TP) was immobilized on Con A-cellulose support and it retained 672 U of TP/g of the matrix [24, 31, 32]. Con A-cellulose bound TP exhibited very high stabilization against the inactivation induced by pH, heat, urea and guanidinium-HCl denaturation.

Several earlier investigators have also reported about the use of Con A support for high yield and stable immobilization of glycoenzymes [31, 33]. Lower concentrations of various detergents enhanced activity of soluble and immobilized TP. Immobilized TP preparation was sufficiently stable against high concentration of several detergents. Such immobilized systems could be used for treatment of hazardous aromatic substances. Enzymatic structure are affected by pollutants in wastewater. Con A cellulose bound TP was remarkably more resistant against the inactivation mediated by DMF, dioxane and n-propanol. Akhtar et al. [24] have demonstrated that bitter gourd peroxidase immobilized on Con A-Sephadex support behaved differently compared to soluble enzyme in aqueous–organic co-solvent mixtures.

Fernandes et al. [34] improved HRP organic solvent tolerance by immobilization. The immobilized soybean seed coat peroxidase exhibited full activity in the presence of organic solvent of concentration range (5-70%, v/v). The soluble form of enzyme was almost inactive in 50% (v/v) of solvents assayed. Enzyme catalysis in organic solvents is possible if structural losses are kept minimum in organic solvents and to achieve such performances from enzymes the Con A- cellulose associated TP seems feasible [35, 36]. Stability to heat, pH, urea, guanidinium-HCl, detergents and several water-miscible organic solvents is remarkable on using Con A-cellulose as matrix to immobilize TP. Immobilization of glycoenzymes on Con A lectin support improves the stability against several denaturants as reported elsewhere and consequently holds potential in wastewater treatment [31, 37].

2.4. Concanavalin A-wood shaving immobilized turnip peroxidase in dye color removal

Wood shaving (WS) is an inexpensive support that finds use in immobilizing enzymes. Bioaffinity support has been prepared using concanavalin A from Jack bean. Salt fractionated turnip peroxidase was immobilized on Con A-WS support. This immobilized protein under varying internal conditions was compared with soluble form in its ability to decolorize direct dyes and its mixtures in batch and continuous reactor system [38]. Con A-WS immobilized TP retained an activity of about 67% as that of initial value. The non-covalent binding of glycoprotein to bioaffinity column adsorbed with Con A is a successful strategy to enhance glycoprotein immobilization. While studying its effectiveness it was observed that immobilized TP (ITP) exhibited a higher dye color removal as compared to soluble forms. Con A-WS served as an excellent bioaffinity column that conferred additional resistance to enzymes in extremes of pH [39]. DR23 and dye mixtures were effectively decolorized by ITP in batch processes at elevated temperatures where as performances were limited to soluble TP. At elevated temperatures the thermal stability improved due adsorption of enzymes with lectin [24, 40].

Dye solutions with sodium chloride (0.5 M) were effectively decolorized by ITP up to 70%. Textile effluents are often contaminated with heavy metals [41, 42]. ITP exhibited better performance in dye color removal of dye solutions containing metal ions suggesting its importance in removal of aromatic pollutants from industrial discharge. The potential of ITP in dye color removal in the presence of 10% and 30% dioxane is excellent. Although soluble enzymes are susceptible to denaturation, ITP showed better catalytic potential as multipoint attachment stabilized the protein structure and prevents the ease of denaturation [39]. Enzymatic catalysis in organic solvents is possible if the organic solvent does not substantially disturb the active site structure [36]. As immobilized enzymes are reusable the processes becomes cost effective. Over 40% of decolorizing activity was still retained when DR23 was treated with eighth repeated use of ITP.

One of the important advantages of immobilized enzyme is its reusability, which influences the cost of industrial applications [24]. Further, the efficiency of ITP was assessed at large scale using two-reactor system [38]. The performance of the reactors was quite efficient as they fulfilled the following requirements: (i) limited accessibility to the immobilized enzyme does not seem to play a role since decolorization by free enzyme was never better than with immobilized preparation [43], (ii) retention of the immobilized enzyme in the reactor in order to maintain an effective operation [44], (iii) maintenance of a good flow rate in order to ensure efficient dye decolorization/degradation [45], and (iv) the performance of the continuous reactor was improved in terms of dye degradation by using activated silica in the second reactor, which helped in the adsorption of toxic reactive species [46].

Water free of dyes (DR 23 and mixture) was obtained when applied on to a double reactor system. ITP present in the first column acted on the dyes which were adsorbed in the second column containing activated silica. The reactors functioned efficiently for over 90 days. In the presence of redox mediator, 1-hydroxybenzotriazole (HOBT); ITP caused significant dye color removal of DR 23 and its mixtures. While studying the absorption spectra it was noticed that the disappearance of peak in the visible region was either due to the removal of pollutants in the form of insoluble products or due the degradation of chromophores in the dyes [24, 47, 48].

The decolorization efficiency of DR 23 and mixtures were different. As compared to individual phenol/dye, biodegradation of complex mixtures of dyes and phenolic compounds were quite slower [24, 49]. One of the possible explanations could be the competition between various phenols/dyes for the enzyme catalytic site or the compounds were recalcitrant and underwent slow transformation. Argument supports the view that industrial effluents containing dyes and its mixtures could be subject to treatment by ITP.

In the presence of ITP the treated polluted water had significantly lower level of TOC (total organic carbon). ITP treated dye solutions exhibited greater loss of TOC. Immobilized HRP removed ~88% of TOC from simulated wastewater containing mixture of chorophenols [50]. Significant amount of TOC from polluted water containing dyes/dye-mixtures and dyeing effluent was removed when treated with soluble and immobilized bitter gourd peroxidase [24]. These findings are suggestive that ITP could be successfully used in removal of dye from effluents of textile, printing and etc.

The support did not showed any signs of physical adsorption of direct dye or mixtures. The dye solution was stable when exposed to bioaffinity support, silica gel, H_2O_2 or enzyme alone. If this is so, than decolorization was an outcome H_2O_2-dependent enzymatic reaction which may involve formation of free radical followed by polymerization and precipitation. The loss of dye color in batch processes was due to removal of aromatic compounds by precipitation. The decrease in aromatic pollutants from the dye solutions was because of adsorption of initial product, free radical compound on the activated silica present in second column.

2.5. β-cyclodextrin-chitosan-horseradish peroxidase (β-CD-chitosan-HRP) complexes for dye color removal

Cyclodextrins (CDs) are formed from the enzymatic degradation of starch by bacteria. These cyclic oligosaccharides containing 6 (α-CD), 7 (β-CD) or 8 (γ-CD) linked with α-(1, 4) linked glucose units. The most important structural features of these compounds include their toroidal shape with an interior cavity that is hydrophobic and exterior hydrophilic [51]. CDs are capable of forming inclusion compounds both in solution and in the solid state with a variety of guest molecules, whereby the guest molecules are placed in their hydrophobic interior cavity [52]. To improve the chemical stability, absorption, bioavailability and controlled release of some drugs the CDs find wide applications in pharmaceutical science [53]. In addition, CDs because of their low production cost have attracted considerable attention in many others fields (e.g., agriculture, nanocomposites, chromatography, biotechnology and bioremediation).

With the progressive adoption of industrial-based lifestyle and the increasing global population have increased the anthropogenic impact on the biosphere. Textile industry discharges hazardous compounds that can seep into aquifers and subsequently contaminate underground water or surface waters. These pollutants of various natures have far reaching impact on aquatic life and human health [54]. These dyes are difficult to remove by conventional wastewater treatment as they possess highly complex chemical structures [55, 56]. The development of enzyme based strategy to treat dyes from wastewater has received much emphasis in recent times [24, 57, 58].

Peroxidases can be used in the detoxification and biotransformation of several aromatic pollutants present in wastewater [4, 59]. HRP was immobilized in very high yield with β-CD-chitosan. The immobilized preparation was highly active and showed a very high effectiveness factor. This method of immobilization was far superior as compared to other strategies [20, 21, 60]. The immobilization of different enzymes with CDs involves forces that are responsible for the stability were ionic, hydrogen, Van der Waals and hydrophobic interactions [61].

At pH 8.0, maximum binding was achieved for HRP with β-CD-chitosan. The adsorption of enzymes on different types of support is pH dependent [35, 62]. Zhu et al. [63] reported a novel immobilization approach based on the supramolecular function between β-CD polymer and HRP in which maximum binding of the enzymes on the support was obtained in a phosphate buffer solution of pH 7.0. It was concluded that the optimization of the enzyme concentration is also of most importance because higher enzyme concentrations shows no significant influence on dye decolorization. The dye color removal by soluble HRP increased as the incubation time was enhanced with maximum achievement after 2 h. There was no significant effect on decolorizing ability on prolonging the time further. On treatment with fenugreek (*Trigonella foenum-graecum* L.) seed peroxidase the textile effluent from the carpet industry decolorized to 68% of original in 2.5 h [64].

At concentrations above 0.6 mM H_2O_2 soluble HRP was inactivated. Buchanan and Nicell [65] had earlier reported the inactivation of peroxidases by higher concentrations of H_2O_2. Once, the substrate is fully consumed, most of the enzyme is expected to react with residual H_2O_2. Therefore, if a treatment process is to be designed in order to reuse residual enzyme activity, it will be necessary to limit the quantity of H_2O_2 supplied during the treatment [66, 67]. The decolorization of the textile effluent is pH dependent because it affects the solubility and concentrations of the counter ions, with subsequent impact on the functional groups of the used reagents and the degree of ionization during reaction. The decolorization of an effluent by soluble calcium alginate-entrapped bitter gourd (*Momordica charantia*) peroxidase; 48% and 71% removal of color were recorded at pH 5.0, by the soluble and immobilized peroxidase respectively [68].

Color removal efficiency by the free and immobilized enzyme preparations increased with increasing temperature; the soluble enzyme exhibits a lower optimal temperature than the immobilized samples. The improvement in thermal stability of the complex may be an outcome of a multipoint complexation of peroxidase with the support. A similar rationale was made to explain why lectin bound enzymes were more stable than the soluble form [68]. The color removal efficiency in a batch process was lower for the soluble form of HRP than the bound enzyme. This may be due to the fact that the immobilized enzyme preparation would be less sensitive to the inactivating metabolites produced from the catalytic reaction, which accumulate in batch processes [69].

Two continuous bed reactors containing both of the immobilized preparations were operated simultaneously for the continuous oxidative removal of azo dye from textile effluent. These reactors had high color removal efficiency. A similar observation reported that the oxidative degradation and removal of endocrine disrupting compound, bisphenol A, in a spiral bed reactor [69]. The spiral bed reactor at operational parameters was functional in oxidative removal of bisphenol A for approximately a month. Immobilized preparations of enzymes have dual advantages of stability as well as reusability. In comparison to uncrosslinked enzymes, the cross-linked preparation retained a remarkable high decolorizing activity. Calcium alginate-starch-entrapped cross-linked bitter gourd peroxidase was shown to polymerize and remove benzidine from model wastewater. Even after its sixth repeated use, the immobilized enzyme was able to catalyzed oxidation and polymerizes 58% of the benzidine [70].

2.6. Immobilized cauliflower (*Brassica oleracea*) bud peroxidase (CBP) on calcium alginate gel beads in dye color removal

Synthetic dyes are difficult to remove from effluents by conventional biological processes as they are highly stable and resistant to microbial attack [71]. Although physico-chemical methods are available for dye color removal but being expensive finds limited application [72]. Another concern of such approaches are the generation of intermediates and end products that are carcinogenic and mostly more toxic than the dyes *per se*. Approaches utilizing biodegradative abilities of some white rot fungi and peroxidases from vegetable sources seems promising [73, 74]. Owing to their extracellular nonspecific free radical-based enzymatic system, they can completely eliminate a variety of xenobiotics as well as synthetic dyes, giving rise to nontoxic compounds [75, 76].

B. oleracea popularly known as cauliflower is widely planted in tropical areas and consumed as vegetables and has earlier been shown by our group to be significantly effective in decolorizing synthetic recalcitrant dye. Salt fractionated immobilized CBP with lectin Con A was entrapped into calcium alginate-pectin beads [77]. Peroxidases in conjunction with hydrogen peroxide can act on specific recalcitrant pollutants to remove them either by precipitation or transformation to often innocuous products. They can change the characteristics of a given waste rendering it more amenable for treatment [78]. Their catalytic action is extremely efficient and selective as opposed to chemical catalysts due to higher reaction rates, milder reaction conditions (relatively low temperature and in the entire aqueous phase pH range) and greater stereo-specificity [79]. Though much attention has been paid in the utilization of biocatalysts in several fields, their involvement has been felt very recently in solving the environmental problems [80, 81]. Soluble enzymes have inherent limitations of losing catalytic potential due structural variations influenced by the complexity of effluents. Immobilization is a way out to improve their catalytic characteristics with enhancement in their reusability. Different polymeric materials have been employed for encapsulation of enzymes and their ability in treating the effluents containing pollutants [82, [83]. However, appropriate selection of encapsulation material specific to the enzyme and optimization of process conditions is still under intensive investigation.

Immobilizing enzymes directly from crude homogenate is relatively a much cheaper approach [84]. Although the immobilized form of bio-molecules holds commercial importance, protocols available for such preparations are limited. Immobilization by adsorption is an effective procedure for binding enzymes directly from partially purified preparations or even from crude homogenates [29]. Calcium alginate mediated entrapment is a simple, economical, effective and sustainable approach for using enzymes either from crude extract or directly from partially purified preparations for detoxification and degradation of phenolic compounds in waste water [24, 39, 77].

Immobilization turns out be an articulated approach as the enzyme activity must not be severely compromised. Where enzymes are glycosylated proteins, the glycosyl moieties can be exploited for immobilization as they are generally not engaged in catalysis. While lectins are useful in characterizing glycoproteins, glycoenzymes have been immobilized on concanavalin A affinity column or as Con A-glycoenzyme complexes [37, 39]. Peroxidase from cauliflower bud is a better choice than other vegetable peroxidases as it is sufficiently thermostable, operates in a wide range of pH, economic and effective with low concentration of redox mediators in decolorizing recalcitrant synthetic dyes [85].

2.6.1. Activity of Soluble and Immobilized CBP

The specific activity of peroxidase preparation increased to 3.5 fold over crude enzyme which exhibited an initial specific activity of 98 U/mg of protein. This enzyme preparation was used for direct immobilization as enzyme–Con A complex. Peroxidases in free form have a better chance to leak out of calcium alginate pectin gel and therefore the leaching of enzymes from porous beads is checked by complexing peroxidases and using the insoluble CBP-Con A complex for entrapping into calcium alginate pectin gel. By selecting these concentrations, encapsulation efficiency increases to 93% and leakage decreases to lower than 6%. With 0.2 ml of Con A, the CBP–Con A complex expressed an activity of 84% which on entrapment into calcium alginate–pectin gel resulted in further decrease (64%) of peroxidase activity. Further, the effect of enzyme loading on entrapped activity was evaluated by entrapping increasing concentration of enzyme. Optimum concentration (512 U/ml) was sufficient for maximum expression of peroxidase activity by entrapped preparation. Pre-immobilized or cross-linked enzymes that remain inside polymeric matrices for longer duration than their soluble counterparts provide higher mechanical and operational stability [19, 86]. It also indicated that enzymes with high molecular mass stay for longer duration inside polymeric matrix. Pre-immobilization increases molecular dimensioning of the enzyme and thereby prevents its leaching from alginate beads.

Immobilized peroxidase preparations exhibited maximum peroxidase activity at 40°C which was true even for soluble counterpart of CBP. However, CBP–Con A and entrapped CBP–Con A complex retained greater fraction of catalytic activity at higher temperatures. A comparative analysis showed that entrapped CBP-Con A expressed 79.6% activity whereas CBP-Con A complex with 62.6% and soluble state 48.4% were relatively poor performers under identical experimental conditions. The peroxidase activity was sufficiently high in the first 1 h for different immobilized forms (79.6% & 89.6% for CBP–Con A complex and entrapped states respectively) whereas a relatively progressive decline was observed with the soluble CBP on prolonging the time duration.

2.6.2. *Activity of CBP under different operational conditions*

2.6.2.1. *Temperature and pH*

Immobilization enhanced the resistance/stability of enzyme to high temperatures. At reasonably high temperatures of 60°C the enzyme expressed 66.6% and 83.7% peroxidase activity as CBP–Con A complex and calcium-alginate entrapped CBP–Con A complex respectively. On increasing the temperature further to 80°C the entrapped immobilized form of CBP exhibited 46.5% peroxidase activity which declined to 31.2% at 90°C. The entrapment of CBP-Con A complex conferred higher retention of its molecular structure and as a result the catalytic activity was improved at elevated temperatures. Such systems could prove useful where operational temperatures are high. As peroxidases are glycoprotein in nature, lectin association immobilizes the molecular conformation by multipoint attachment contributing to stability and thus serves even better when entrapped in calcium-alginate pectin gel [28]. pH activity profile of soluble CBP, CBP–Con A and entrapped CBP–Con A was evaluated by incubating these preparations in the buffers of varying pH values (2.0–9.0). The pH range 4.0–6.0 was sufficient for optimum enzyme activity. While comparing the activity in varying pH medium, it was noticed that immobilized preparations were more stable at pH 4; whereas soluble CBP exhibited a maximum activity (96%) at pH 5.0 which declined in alkaline medium. Interestingly, immobilized CBP could withstand wide alkaline medium in comparison to soluble forms. This broadening in pH-activity suggested that entrapment of enzymes in gel beads provides a microenvironment for enzyme, which may play an important role in the state of protonation / deprotonation of protein molecules [29]. Formation of CBP–Con A complex promotes retention of molecular structure and consequently confers additional resistance to enzyme against extreme conditions of pH [24, 87].

2.6.2.2. *Denaturants*

Urea (4.0 M) is a strong denaturant of some proteins and it irreversibly denatures soluble CBP [88]. Upon subjecting the soluble and immobilized CBP preparation to urea entrapped CBP-Con A complex retained profound activity with progressive increase in the incubation time. The free enzyme lost almost 78% of initial activity, whereas in case of CBP-Con A complex the activity diminished by 35% under identical experimental conditions.

The mechanism of urea induced denaturation is not completely understood. However, it is suggested that protein molecule unfolds by direct interaction of urea molecule via non-covalent interactions with the peptide backbone. The peptide backbone essentially contributes to the structure of the molecule and therefore the loss of structure results in the loss of catalytic activity [24, 29]. Fatima and Husain [89] have reported the enhancement of resistance to denaturation by complexing glycoenzymes with lectin like Con A. In the presence of lower concentration of dioxane the free and immobilized states of enzymes showed over 60% of peroxidase activity. However, the activity manifested by immobilized counterparts was sufficiently higher. With higher concentration of dioxane (60% v/v) soluble enzyme retained only 29.8% while CBP–Con A complex and entrapped CBP– Con A retained nearly 41.6% and 54.1% of their actual activity, respectively. It was interesting to note that at even higher concentration of dioxane (80% v/v) soluble form of CBP lost 92% peroxidase activity as compared to immobilized and entrapped CBP-Con A complex exhibiting 29.9% and 48.2% respectively.

Enzyme catalysis is affected by the presence of water miscible organic solvents. As the wastewater is often contaminated by organic pollutants hence the stability of CBP preparations against some water miscible organic solvents needs to be explored. It was observed that entrapped CBP–Con A complex retained remarkably high stabilization against inactivation caused by dioxane and DMF as compared to soluble CBP and CBP–Con A complex. This is substantiated by earlier findings that bioaffinity bound enzymes were significantly more stable likely due to decrease in flexibility and increased molecular rigidity against exposure to water miscible organic solvents [24].

Immobilized peroxidases are reported to be significantly stabilized against denaturation induced by some commonly used detergents (Triton X 100, Tween 20, SDS) [29]. The immobilization of protein by attachment to matrix is sufficient enough to accords protection from denaturation mediated by organic solvents. Moreover, the stabilization of immobilized enzymes against various forms of water-miscible organic solvents could perhaps be due to low water requirement or enhanced rigidity of the enzyme structure. In organic solvents enzymes can perform catalytic activity if the organic solvent does not adversely alter the active site conformation [36].

A number of studies have already been performed on the inhibitory effect of such compounds such as horseradish peroxidase where sodium azide has been shown to be a potent inhibitor of many heme protein-catalyzed reactions [90]. While the effect of sodium azide, on enzyme was adverse, ethylenediamine tetra-acetic acid showed no significant effect on the activity of soluble and immobilized CBP even when its concentration was raised 30 mM. Peroxidase in the presence of sodium azide and H_2O_2 mediates one electron oxidation of azide ions forming azidyl free radicals which bind covalently to the heme moiety of peroxidase, thus inhibiting the enzyme activity [91]. EDTA did not have any significant effect on the activity of CBP and such an observation on enzyme activity has already been reported [92].

The chemical contamination of water by a wide range of toxic derivatives, particularly, heavy metals are a serious environmental problem owing to their potential human toxicity. In view of their presence in wastewater, it became necessary to evaluate the effect of some heavy metals on the activity of CBP. Our results revealed that CBP exhibited more resistance to heavy metal induced inhibition; a concentration-dependent gradual inhibition of CBP activity by $HgCl_2$ was observed. Some recent reports indicated that horseradish peroxidase was remarkably inhibited by heavy metal ions [42, 93].

However, the inhibition of immobilized CBP by $HgCl_2$ was quite low as compared to the soluble enzyme. Although, metals induce conformational changes in enzymes, however peroxidases remain active even in the presence of a number of metal ions, as a part of their detoxifying role. The effect of different metal ions on the activity of different enzymes is related to their affinity to different functional groups present in the enzymatic structure [94, 95]. The stability of immobilized CBP against several metal compounds showed that such enzyme preparations could be exploited for the treatment of aromatic pollutants even in the presence of heavy metals.

2.6.2.3. *Kinetics*

The kinetic parameters of soluble and immobilized CBP were determined using different concentrations of o-dianisidine HCl. The plot of initial enzyme activity versus different concentrations of o-dianisidine HCl for both the enzyme preparations followed a hyperbolic pattern as expected according to the Michaelis–Menton kinetics. Lineweaver–Burk plots of soluble and immobilized CBP were also found to be linear and Michaelis– Menton constant, K_m, for soluble and entrapped CBP–Con A complex was 0.076 and 0.089 mM, respectively. The Vmax values for soluble and immobilized CBP were found to be 22.4 and 16.6 mM/min, respectively. Vmax of soluble enzymes was more than that of immobilized states, although K_m values were closely related. Thus, the immobilization of CBP-Con A complex by entrapment using calcium alginate pectin did not affect the conformation of enzyme, however the accessibility for the substrate was slightly altered.

Glutaraldehyde crosslinking enhances the structural rigidity of protein and also maintains the native structure [96]. The structural rigidity and consequently the native structure of a protein is enhanced by crosslinking [96]. Immobilization by entrapment serves similar functions due to which the CBP becomes more resistant to environment. Since the entrapment of CBP–Con A complex is non-specific and masking of certain amino acids at or near the active site contributed towards lesser formation of enzyme-substrate complex, a decrease in V_{max} was observed in the case of immobilized enzyme preparation. It is well documented that the K_m values of several immobilized enzymes were either unaltered or exhibited minor alteration as compared to those of their respective soluble counterparts.

2.6.2.4. *CBP and dye decolorization*

Entrapped immobilized CBP decolorized 93.7% and 88.2% of DR 19 and mixture of dyes (DR19+DB9) after 2 h of incubation, respectively. Immobilized CBP was more effective as compared to its soluble counterpart in the decolorization of both DR 19 and mixture of dyes. The decolorization achieved by entrapped Con A-CBP complex was reasonably higher for DR19 and dye mixture (DR19+DB9), respectively after 20 days. Even after operation of the two-reactor system for 120 d and 80 d decolorization achieved for DR19 and disperse dye mixture was 64.8% and 56.8% respectively. In the presence of redox mediator, riboflavin the loss of color was significant for both DR19 and dye mixtures. The enzyme catalyzed the breakdown of chromophoric groups present in dyes [47].

In case of continuous reactors TOC decreased significantly on treatment of polluted water with immobilized CBP. The significant loss of TOC from wastewater indicates that the major toxic compounds may have been eliminated from the treated samples. Akhtar and Husain [97] have reported that significant amount of TOC was removed from water polluted with dyes/dye-mixtures and dye effluents on treatment with soluble and immobilized bitter gourd peroxidases. These evidences strongly proved that immobilized CBP–Con A complex could be successfully used for the removal of dye effluents loaded with recalcitrant synthetic dyes.

2.6.2.5. Reusability of Immobilized Enzymes

The immobilized enzyme could be easily removed and assessed for its left over catalytic activity. To demonstrate the reusability of encapsulated enzyme, capsules were separated after 120 min of reaction time and then rinsed thoroughly with distilled water. After 5 times of repeated use test, the dye removal efficiency was reduced to 67.9% for DR 19 and 63.5% for dye mixture (DR 19+DB 9). This efficiency showed progressive decrease with the increase in the cycle numbers. This downfall in the catalytic efficiency might be an outcome of the plugging of the pore membrane and accumulation of radicals in the interior of each capsule which entraps the enzyme active site that leads to the inactivation of enzyme molecules.

While inorganic compounds require acidic conditions to be effective, they may increase costs associated with initial pH of waste waters, corrosion of hardware during treatment and pH neutralization of wastes prior to their release. Enzyme based catalysis reflects preference over intact organisms (containing a multitude of enzymes) because the isolated enzymes act with greater specificity, thereby allowing specific group of pollutants to be targeted for treatment; their potency can be better standardized, they are easier to handle and store and enzyme concentration is not dependent on bacterial growth rates. Enzymes are naturally occurring chemical species and our source comprises of readily renewable resources. Moreover, in contrast to many other enzymes, CBP retains its catalytic activity over wide ranges of temperature, pH, contaminant concentration, consequently making it particularly suitable for application in industrial environment. In addition unlike other enzymes with similar functions CBP is relatively non-specific in terms of its organic substrates, making it applicable for treatment of large variety of aromatic pollutants.

A critical aspect that governs and probably limits the industrial applications of enzymes is inactivation through mechanical, chemical and thermal processes that interact to influence enzyme activity. In particular inactivation of CBP can result from oxidation of the enzyme to inactive forms, phenoxy radical inhibition and adsorption and/or entrapment of the enzyme in precipitating polymers. Therefore reducing the cost of the catalysts has been the focus of much attention. The catalytic lifetimes of pointed gourd peroxidase as well as CBP improves significantly when the reaction is conducted at the optimal pH, temperature while maintaining a low instantaneous enzyme concentration [85]. The efficiency of the crude enzyme preparation was independent of its purity as earlier reported by Alberti and Klibanov [98]. By immobilization using entrapment on calcium alginate pectin beads, the apparent rate of enzyme inactivation was reduced which allowed a significant reduction in enzyme requirements for treatment. This increase in enzyme lifetime represents a very significant saving in terms of treatment costs.

2.7. Diethylaminoethyl Cellulose Immobilized Pointed Gourd (*Trichosanthes dioica*) Peroxidase (PGP) in Decolorization of Synthetic Dyes

PGP cross-linked with glutaraldehyde and adsorbed on DEAE cellulose was efficient in catalyzing the dye color removal of disperse dyes viz., DR19 and dye mixture (DR19+DB9) [99, 100, 101]. Immobilized PGP (I-PGP) was reusable up to seven times to decolorize DR19 and dye mixture to over 50% in comparison to free enzymes. The immobilized states of enzymes are relatively easier to handle and can be stored for longer durations. Immobilized states of PGP have better storage stability and can be used in reactors for the treatment of effluents containing phenolic and other aromatic pollutants including dyes which are predominantly present in textile effluents. The findings on reusability and storage ability suggests that the use of cheaper source of enzyme and support will definitely minimize the cost of immobilization and would provide a suitable strategy for treatment of huge volumes of wastewater in continuous as well as batch processes.

The peroxidases functions better in the presence of redox mediator. Thus it's essential that the enzyme catalytic activity is effective in conjunction with redox mediators and optimum concentration of hydrogen peroxide [102, 103]. The enzymes work well in acidic pH generally in the range of 3 to 6. The findings indicate that immobilized enzymes at operational pH catalyze sufficient dye color removal. The presence of redox mediators enhances the enzymatic dye color removal. Perhaps a correlation exists between redox potential and dye reduction rates. The closer the redox potential is between dye and redox mediator, the faster is dye reduction, because electron transfer is facilitated due to the low potential difference. Such behavior explains the better catalytic properties of riboflavin. However, dye reduction rate is not only determined by redox potential, but also by other factors such as chemical structure, environmental conditions and anaerobic sludge affinity and concentration. The chromophore cleavage by PGP in conjunction with redox mediators was favorable for azo dyes, because the reduction occurs in the nitrogen bonds, which have more affinity to receive electrons, based on electronegative properties, as compared to carbon-carbon bond chromophore of the anthraquinone dyes. Therefore, the effect of redox mediators on dye reduction is related to the molecular structure, being more evident for azo dyes with low decolorization rates in the absence of these compounds, and ineffective for anthraquinone dyes because of the structural stability of the latter [102].

Immobilized peroxidase was much more effective in removing dye color as compared to soluble enzyme in a batch process. A possible reason could be that immobilization shielded the number of reactive free amino groups, which are not protected in soluble case and hence, were more susceptible to reaction with the reactive products like free radicals [50]. Our findings are in accordance to our earlier studies using immobilized PGP-Concanavalin A complex on calcium alginate pectin gel in decolorization of synthetic dyes [29]. To evaluate the efficiency of immobilized PGP on a large scale for the removal of dye color, a vertical continuous reactor system was designed and operated continuously with a flow rate of 15 mL h^{-1}. The reactors worked for more than 60 d approximately, thus explaining their efficiency towards dye decolorization. A significant loss of color appeared when DR19 or mixture of dyes was treated with I- PGP in the presence of redox mediator, riboflavin in a continuous reactor system.

3. Conclusion

The preparation and application of immobilized enzymes has received greater attention in recent times. The experimental results obtained revealed the effectiveness of the immobilized peroxidases in sustainable dye color removal and remediation of other toxic pollutants. The immobilized preparations exhibited adequate storage stability and protein content. The immobilization confers a shielding effect on peroxidases against inactivation and/or inhibition and therefore, higher dye color removal can be reached with the same concentration of immobilized preparation as soluble peroxidases. The performance of dye color removal was found to be highly dependent on enzyme dose, hydrogen peroxidases, temperature and aqueous pH. The encapsulated enzyme activity shows higher relative activity in acidic solutions over a broader range which are the most common conditions appeared in waste stream. Enzyme retention activity, encapsulation and leakage percentage of enzymes are influenced by gel preparation condition and finding a proper value for above quantities totally depends on the used support. The reusability experiment showed that these biocatalysts can be used up to several cycles without serious deficiency in their catalytic performance. A two-reactor system with simple operational protocol for decolorization /degradation of disperse dyes can be designed for the potential future use of immobilized peroxidases. Interestingly, the described system is developed with a cheaper biocatalyst and support matrix that is quite effective in treating dyes continuously. Thus, immobilized peroxidase preparations could be exploited for developing bioreactors for the treatment of phenolic and other aromatic pollutants including synthetic dyes present in industrial effluents.

References

[1] Jamal, F. (2011). Functional Suitability of Soluble Peroxidases from Easily Available Plant Sources in decolorization of synthetic dyes. In: Advances in Treating Textile Effluent, Prof. Peter Hauser (Ed.), InTech, ISBN: 978-953-307-704-8, pp. 49-72.

[2] Jamal, F. & Khan, M.Y. (2011). Peroxidases and redox mediators in dye catalysis and detoxification of industrial effluents. In: Catalysis: Principles, Types and Applica-

tions, Minsuh Song (Ed.), Nova Science Publishers, Inc. ISBN 978-1-61209-654-4, pp. 1-35.

[3] Batra, R. & Gupta, M.N. (1994a). Enhancement of enzyme-activity in aqueous-organic solvent mixtures. Biotechnol. Lett. 16, 1059–1064, ISSN: 0141-5492.

[4] Dur′an, N., Rosa, M. D'Annibale, A. & Gianfreda, L. (2002). Applications of Laccase and Tyrosinases (Phenoloxidases) immobilized on different support: A review. Enzyme Microb. Technol, 31, 907–931, ISSN: 0141-0229.

[5] Yagar, H. & Sagiroglu, A. (2002). Non-covalent immobilization of quince (*Cydonia oblonga*) polyphenol oxidase. Acta Chim. Slov. 49, 893–902, ISSN: 1318-0207.

[6] Shan, D., Mousty, C. & Cosnier, S. (2004). Subnanomolar cyanide detection at polyphenol oxidase/clay biosensors. Anal. Chem, 76, 178–183, ISSN: 0003-2700.

[7] Khan, A.A., Akhtar, S. & Husain, Q. (2005). Adsorption of polyphenol oxidases on Celite 545 directly from ammonium sulphate fractionated proteins of brinjal (*Solanum melongena*). J. Sci. Ind. Res, 64, 621–626, ISSN: 0022-4456.

[8] Davis, S. & Burns, R. (1990). Decolorization of phenolic effluents by soluble and immobilized phenol oxidases. Appl. Microb. Biotechnol. 32, 721–726, ISSN: 0175-7598.

[9] Reyes, P., Pickard, M.A., Varzquez-Duhalt, R., Hydroxybenzotriazole increases the range of textile dyes decolorized by immobilized laccase. Biotechnol. Lett. 21 (1999) 875–880, ISSN: 0141-5492.

[10] huttleworth, K.L. & Bollag, J. M. (1986). Soluble and immobilized laccase as catalysts for the transformation of substituted phenols. Enzyme Microb. Technol, 8, 171–177, ISSN: 0141-0229.

[11] Fling, M., Horowitz, N.H. & Heinemann, S.F. (1963). The isolation and properties of crystalline tyrosinase from *Neurospora*. J. Biol. Chem, 238, 2045–2053, ISSN: 0021-9258.

[12] Partington, J.C. & Bolwell, G.P. (1996). Purification of polyphenol oxidase free of the storage protein patatin from potato tuber. Phytochemistry, 42, 1499–1502, ISSN: 0031-9422.

[13] Khan, A.A., Akhtar, S., Husain, Q., (2006) Direct immobilization of polyphenol oxidases on Celite 545 from ammonium sulphate fractionated proteins of potato (*Solanum tuberosum*). J. Mol. Catal. B: Enzy, 40, 58-63, ISSN: 0923-9820.

[14] Leontievsky, A.A., Myasoedova, N.M., Baskunov, B.P., Golovleva, L.A., Bucke, C. & Evans, C.S. (2001). Transformation of 2,4,6-trichlorophenol by free and immobilized fungal laccase. Appl. Microb. Biotechnol, 57, 85–91, ISSN: 0175-7598.

[15] Anderson, W.A., Bay, P., Legge, R.L. & Moo-Young, M. (1990) Adsorption of Streptococcus faecalis on diatomite carriers for use in biotransformations J. Chem. Technol. Biotechnol, 47, 93–100, ISSN: 1097-4660.

[16] Moore, B.M. & Flurkey, W.H., (1990). Sodium dodecyl sulfate activation of a plant polyphenoloxidase. J. Biol. Chem, 265, 4982–4988, ISSN: 0021-9258.

[17] Jimenez, M. & Garcia-Carmona, F. (1996). The effect of sodium dodecyl sulfate on polyphenol oxidase. Phytochemistry, 42, 1503–1509, ISSN: 0031-9422.

[18] Batra, R. & Gupta, M.N. (1994b). Noncovalent immobilization of potato (*Solanum – tuberosum*) polyphenol oxidase on chitin. Biotechnol. Appl. Biochem, 19, 209–215, ISSN: 1470-8744.

[19] Kulshrestha, Y. & Husain, Q. (2006a). Direct immobilization of peroxidase on DEAE cellulose from ammonium sulphate fractionated proteins of bitter gourd (*Momordica charantia*) Enzyme Microb. Technol, 38, 470–477, ISSN: 0141-0229.

[20] Levy, I., Ward, G., Hadar, Y., Shoseyov, O. & Dosoretz, C.G. (2003). Oxidation of 4-bromophenol by the recombinant fused protein cellulose-binding domain horseradish peroxidase immobilized on cellulose. Biotechnol. Bioeng, 82, 223-231, ISSN: 1097-0290.

[21] Shaffiqu, T.S., Roy, J.J., Nair, R.A., Abraham, T.E., 2002. Degradation of textile dyes mediated by plant peroxidases. Applied Biochemistry and Biotechnology 6, 315-326, ISSN: 0273-2289.

[22] Reddy, R.C.K., Srivastava, P.K., Dey, P.M. & Kayastha, A.M. (2004). Immobilization of pigeon pea (*Cajanus cajan*) urease on DEAE cellulose paper strips for urea estimation. Biotechnol. Appl. Biochem, 39, 323–327, ISSN: 0885-4513.

[23] Strauss, U.T., Kandelbauer, A. & Faber, K. (2000). Stabilization and activity enhancement of mandelate racemase from Peudomonas putida ATCC 12336 by immobilization. Biotechnol. Lett, 22, 515–520, ISSN: 0141-5492.

[24] Akhtar, S., Khan, A.A. & Husain, Q. (2005). Simultaneous purification and immobilization of bitter gourd (*Momordica charantia*) peroxidases on bioaffinity support. J. Chem. Technol. Biotechnol, 80, 198–205, ISSN: 1097-4660.

[25] Mozhaev, V.V., Seregeeva, M.V., Belova, A.B. & Khmelnitsky, Y.L. (1990). Multipoint attachment to a support protect enzyme from inactivation by organic solvents: alpha chymotrypsin in aqueous solution of alcohol and diols. Biotechnol. Bioeng, 35, 653–659, ISSN: 1097-0290.

[26] Fernandez-Lafuente, R., Wood, A.N.P. & Cowan, D.A. (1995). Reducing enzyme conformation flexibility by multipoint covalent immobilization. Biotechnol. Tech, 9, 1–6, ISSN: 0951-208X.

[27] Jan, U., Husain, Q. & Saleemuddin, M. (2001). Preparation of stable, highly active and immobilized glucose oxidase using the anti-enzyme antibodies and $F(ab)'_2$. Biotechnol. Appl. Biochem, 34, 13–17, ISSN: 1470-8744.

[28] Jan, U. & Husain, Q. (2004). Preparation of highly stable, very active and high yield multilayered assembly of glucose oxidase by using carbohydrate specific polyclonal antibodies. Biotechnol. Appl. Biochem, 39, 233–239, ISSN: 1470-8744.

[29] Musthapa, M.S., Akhtar, S., Khan, A.A. & Husain, Q. (2004). An economical, simple and high yield procedure for the immobilization/stabilization of peroxidases from turnip roots. J. Sci. Ind. Res, 63: 540-547, ISSN: 0022-4456.

[30] Sakharov, I.Y., Castillo, J.L., Areza, J.C. & Galaev, I.Y. (2000). Purification and stability of peroxidase of African oil palm *Elaies guineensis*. Bioseparation, 9, 125–132, ISSN: 0923-179X.

[31] Saleemuddin, M., Husain, Q., 1991. Concanavalin A: an useful ligand for glycoenzyme immobilization—a review. Enzyme Microb. Technol, 13, 290–295, ISSN: 0141-0229.

[32] Husain, S., Husain, Q. & Saleemuddin, M. (1992). Inactivation and reactivation of horseradish peroxidase immobilized by variety of procedures. Ind. J. Biochem. Biophys, 29, 482–486, ISSN: 0301-1208.

[33] Saleemuddin, M., 1999. Bioaffinity based immobilization of enzymes. Adv. Biochem. Eng. Biotechnol, 64, 203–226, ISSN: 0724-6145.

[34] Fernandes, K.F., Lima, C.S., Pinho, H. & Collins, C.H. (2003). Immobilization of horseradish peroxidase onto polyaniline polymers. Proc. Biochem. 38, 1379–1384, ISSN: 1359-5113.

[35] Magri, M.L., Miranda, M.V. & Cascone, O. (2005). Immobilization of soybean seed coat peroxidase on polyaniline: synthesis optimization and catalytic properties. Biocatal. Biotransformation, 23, 339-346, ISSN: 1024-2422.

[36] Ryu, K. & Dordick, J. (1992). How do organic solvents affect peroxidase structure and function. Biochemistry, 31, 2588–2598, ISSN: 0006-2960.

[37] Mislovicova, D.P., Gemeiner, P., Sandula, J., Masarova, J., Vikartovska, A. & Doloomansky, P. (2000). Examination of bioaffinity immobilization by precipitation of mannan and mannan-containing enzymes with legume lectins. Biotechnol. Appl. Biochem. 31, 153–159, ISSN: 0885-4513.

[38] Matto, M. & Husain, Q. (2009). Decolorization of direct dyes by immobilized turnip peroxidase in batch and continuous processes. Ecotoxicol. Environ. Saf, 72, 965–971, ISSN: 0147-6513.

[39] Kulshrestha, Y. & Husain, Q. (2006b). Bioaffinity-based an inexpensive and high yield procedure for the immobilization of turnip (*Brassica rapa*) peroxidase. Biomol. Eng, 23, 291–297, ISSN: 1389-0344.

[40] Matto, M. & Husain, Q. (2006). Entrapment of porous and stable Con A-peroxidase complex into hybrid calcium alginate-pectin gel. J. Chem. Technol. Biotechnol, 81, 1316–1323, ISSN: 1097-4660.

[41] Hatvani, N. & Mecs, I. (2003). Effects of certain heavy metals on the growth, dye decolorization, and enzyme activity ofLentinula edodes. Ecotoxicol. Environ. Saf, 55, 199–203, ISSN: 0147-6513.

[42] Einollahi, N., Abbasi, S., Dashti, N. & Vaezzadeh, F. (2006). Effect of mercuric chloride on kinetic properties of horseradish peroxidase. Iran. J. Publ. Health, 35, 49–56, ISSN: 2251-6085.

[43] Kandelbauer, A., Maute, O., Kessler, R.W., Erlacher, A. & Gu°bitz, G.M. (2004). Study of dye decolorization in an immobilized laccase enzyme-reactor using online spectroscopy. Biotechnol. Bioeng, 87, 552–563, ISSN: 1097-0290.

[44] Lopez, C., Mielgo, I., Moreira, M.T., Feijoo, G. & Lema, J.M. (2002). Enzymatic membrane reactors for biodegradation of recalcitrant compounds: application to dye decolourisation. J. Biotechnol. 29, 249–257, ISSN: 0168-1656.

[45] Palmieri, G., Giardina, P. & Sannia, G. (2005). Laccase-mediated Remazol Brilliant Blue R decolorization in a fixed-bed bioreactor. Biotechnol. Prog, 21, 1436–1441, ISSN: 1520-6033.

[46] Azni, I. & Katayon, S. (2003). Possible utilization of silica gel sludge for the removal of phenol from aqueous solutions: laboratory studies. Environmentalist, 23, 329–334, ISSN: 0251-1088.

[47] Moreira, M.T., Palma, C., Mielgo, I., Feijoo, G. & Lema, J.M. (2001). In vitro degradation of a polymeric dye (Poly R-478) by manganese peroxidase. Biotechnol. Bioeng. 75, 362–368, ISSN: 1097-0290.

[48] Bhunia, A., Durani, S. & Wangikar, P.P. (2001). Horseradish peroxidase catalyzed degradation of industrially important dyes. Biotechnol. Bioeng, 72, 562–567, ISSN: 1097-0290.

[49] Kahru, A., Pollumaa, L., Reiman, R., Ratsep, A., Luders, M. & Maloveryan, A. (2000). The toxicity and biodegradation of eight main phenolic compounds characteristic to the oil-shale industry wastewater: a test battery approach. Environ. Toxicol, 15, 431–442, ISSN: 1552-8618.

[50] Tatsumi, K., Wada, S. & Ichikawa, H. (1996). Removal of chlorophenols from wastewater by immobilized horseradish peroxidase. Biotechnol. Bioeng, 51, 126-130, ISSN: 1097-0290.

[51] Szejtli, J. (1982). Cyclodextrins and their inclusion complexes. Starch, 34, 395-401, ISSN: 0038-9056.

[52] Nakai, Y., Yamamoto, K., Terada, K. & Watanabe, D. (1987). New methods for preparing cyclodextrin inclusion compounds I; Heating in a sealed container. Chem. Pharm. Bull, 35, 4609-4617, ISSN: 0009-2363.

[53] Duchene, D. & Wouessidjewe, D. (1990). Pharmaceuticals uses of cyclodextrins and derivates. Drug Dev. Ind. Pharm, 16, 175-182, ISSN: 0363-9045.

[54] Ashoka, C., Geetha, M.S. & Sullia, S.B. (2002). Bioleaching of composite textile dye effluent using bacterial consortia. Asian J. Microbiol. Biotechnol. Environ. Sci, ISSN: 4, 65-68, ISSN: 0972-3005.

[55] Husain, Q. (2006). Potential applications of the oxidoreductive enzymes in the decolorization and detoxification of textile and other synthetic dyes from polluted water. Crit. Rev. Biotechnol, 26, 201-221, ISSN: 0738-8551.

[56] Murugesan, K., Nam, I.H., Kim, Y.M. & Chang, Y.S. (2007). Decolorization of reactive dyes by a thermostable laccase produced by *Ganoderma lucidum* in solid state culture. Enzyme Microb. Techol, 40, 1662-1672, ISSN: 0141-0229.

[57] Christian, V.V., Shrivastava, R., Novotny, C. & Vyas, B.R. (2003). Decolorization of sulfonaphthalein dyes by manganese peroxidase activity of the white-rot fungus *Phanerochaete chrysosporium*. Folia Microbiologica, 48, 771-774, ISSN: 0015-5632.

[58] Mielgo, I., Lopez, C., Moreira, M.T., Feijoo, G. & Lema, J.M. (2003). Oxidative degradation of azo dyes by manganese peroxidase under optimized conditions. Biotechnol. Prog, 19, 325-331, ISSN: 8756-7938.

[59] Torres, E., Bustos-Jaimes, I. & Le-Borgne, S. (2003). Potential use of oxidative enzymes for the detoxification of organic pollutants. Appl. Cat. B- Environ, 46, 1-15, ISSN: 0926-3373.

[60] Muller, J. & Zwing, T. (1982). An experimental verification of the theory of diffusion limitation of immobilized enzymes. Biochim. Biophys. Acta, 705, 117-123, ISSN: 0006-3002

[61] Felici, M., Marza-Perez, M., Hatzakis, N.S., Nolte, R.J.M. & Feiters, M.C. (2008). β- cyclodextrin appended giant amphiphile: aggregation to vesicle polymersomes and immobilisation of enzymes. Chem. Eur. J, 14, 9914-9920, ISSN: 0947-6539.

[62] Ansari, S.A. & Husain, Q. (2010). Lactose hydrolysis byb-galactosidase immobilized on concanavalin A-cellulose in batch and continuous mode. J. Mol. Cat. B: Enzym, 6, 68-74, ISSN: 0923-9820.

[63] Zhu, M., Han, S. & Yuan, Z. (2000). β-cyclodextrin polymer as the immobilized matrix for peroxidase and mediator in the fabrication of a sensor for hydrogen peroxide. J. Electroanal. Chem, 480, 255-261, ISSN: 1572-6657.

[64] Husain, Q., Karim, Z. & Banday, Z.Z. (2010). Decolorization of textile effluent by soluble fenugreek (*Trigonella foenum-graecum* L) seeds peroxidase. Water Air Soil Pollut, 212, 319-328, ISSN: 0049-6979.

[65] Buchanan, I.D. & Nicell, J.A. (1997). Model development for horseradish peroxidase catalyzed removal of aqueous phenol. Biotechnol. Bioeng, 54, 251-261, ISSN: 1097-0290.

[66] Hong-Mei, L. & Nicell, J.A. (2008). Biocatalytic oxidation of bisphenol A in a reverse micelle system using horseradish peroxidase. Bioresour. Technol, 99, 4428-4437, ISSN: 0960-8524.

[67] Karim, Z. & Husain, Q. (2009). Redox-mediated oxidation and removal of aromatic amines from polluted water by partially purified bitter gourd (*Momordica charantia*) peroxidase. Int. Biodeter. Biodeg, 63, 587-593, ISSN: 0964-8305.

[68] Karim, Z. & Husain, Q. (2010). Removal of anthracene from model wastewater by immobilized peroxidase from *Momordica charantia* in batch process as well as in a continuous spiral-bed reactor. J. Mol. Catal. B: Enzy, 66, 302-310, ISSN: 0923-9820.

[69] Karim, Z. & Husain, Q. (2011). Removal of benzidine from polluted water by soluble and immobilized peroxidase in batch processes and continuous horizontal bed reactor. Environ. Technol, 32, 83-91, ISSN: 0959-3330.

[70] Pala, A. & Toket, E. (2002). Color removal from cotton textile industry wastewater by an activated sludge system with various additives. Water Res, 36, 2922–2925, ISSN: 0043-1354.

[71] Moreira, M.T., Melgo, I., Feijoo, G. & Lema, J.M. (2000). Evaluation of different fungal strains in the decolorization of synthetic dye. Biotechnol. Lett, 22, 1499-1503, ISSN: 0141-5492.

[72] Liu, W., Chao, Y., Yang, X., Buo, H. & Qian, S. (2004). Biodecolourization of azo, anthraquinonic and triphenylmethane dyes by white-rot fungi and a laccase secreting engineered strain. J. Ind. Microbiol. Biotechnol, 31, 127-132, ISSN: 1367-5435.

[73] Jamal, F., Qidwai, T., Singh, D., Pandey, P.K. (2012). Biocatalytic activity of immobilized pointed gourd (*Trichosanthes dioica*) peroxidase -concanavalin A complex on calcium alginate pectin gel. J. Mol. Catal. B: Enzy, 74, 125-131, ISSN: 0923-9820.

[74] Bezalel, L., Hadar, Y. & Cerniglia, C.E. (1997). Enzymatic mechanisms involved in phenanthrene degradation by the white rot fungus *Pleurotus ostreatus*. Appl. Environ. Microbiol, 63, 2495-2501, ISSN: 0099-2240.

[75] Pointing, S.B. (2001). Feasibility of bioremediation by white-rot fungi. Appl. Microbiol. Biotechnol, 57, 20–23, ISSN: 0175-7598.

[76] Jamal, F., Singh, S., Qidwai, T., Singh, D., Pandey, P.K. & Khan, M.Y. (2013). Catalytic activity of soluble versus immobilized cauliflower (*Brassica oleracea*) bud peroxidase-

concanavalin A complex and its application in dye color removal. Biocatal. Agri. Biotechnol, 2, 311-321, ISSN: 1878-8181.

[77] Kasam, J. & Niceu, J.A. (1997). Potential application of enzymes in waste treatment. J. Chem. Tech. Biotechnol, 69, 141–153, ISSN: 0268-2575.

[78] Mohan, S.V., Prasad, K.K., Prakasham, R.S. & Sarma, P.N. (2002). Enzymatic pretreatment to enhance the biodegradability of industrial wastewater. Chem. Wkly, 23, 163–168, ISSN: 0045-6500.

[79] Mohan, S.V., Prasad, K.K., Roa, N.C. & Sarma, P.N. (2005). Acid azo dye degradation by free and immobilized horseradish peroxidase (HRP) catalyzed process. Chemosphere, 58, 1097-2005, ISSN: 0045-6535.

[80] Nicell, J.A. (1994). Kinetics of horseradish peroxidase-catalysed polymerization and precipitation of aqueous 4-chlorophenol. J. Chem. Technol. Biotechnol. 60, 203–5, ISSN: 1097-4660.

[81] Zille, A., Tzanov, T., Gubitz, G.M. & Cavaco-Paulo, A. (2003). Immobilized laccase for decolorization of Reactive Black 5 dyeing effluent. Biotechnol. Lett. 25, 1473–1477, ISSN: 0141-5492.

[82] Rogalski, J., Jozwik, E., Hatakka, A., Leonomicz, A., 1995. Immobilization of laccase from *Phlebia radiata* on controlled porosity glass. J. Mol. Catal. B: Enzy, 95, 99-108, ISSN: 0923-9820.

[83] Gupta, M.N. & Mattiason, B. (1992). Unique application of immobilized proteins in bioanalytical systems. Meth. Biochem. Anal, 36, 1–4, ISSN: 0076-6941.

[84] Jamal, F., Qidwai, T., Singh, D. & Pandey, P.K. (2011). Catalytic potential of cauliflower (*Brassica oleracea*) bud peroxidase in decolorization of synthetic recalcitrant dyes using redox mediator. Catal. Commun, 15, 93–98, ISSN: 1566-7367.

[85] Betancor, L., Lopez-Gallego, F., Hidalgo, A., Fuentes, M., Podrasky, O., Kuncova, G., Guisan, J.M. & Fernandez-Lafuente, R. (2005). Advantages of the preimmobilization of enzymes on porous supports for their entrapment in sol–gels. Biomacromolecules, 6 1027-1030, ISSN: 1525-7797.

[86] Lopez, C., Moreira, M.T., Feijoo, G. & Lema, J.M. (2004). Dye decolorization by manganese peroxidase in an enzymatic membrane bioreactor. Biotechnol. Prog, 20, 74-81, ISSN: 1520-6033.

[87] Makhatadze, G.I. & Privalor, P.I. (1992). Protein interactions with urea and guanidinium hydrochloride: a calorimetric study. J. Mol. Biol, 226, 491–495, ISSN: 0022-2836.

[88] Fatima, A. & Husain, Q. (2007). A role of glycosyl moieties in the stabilization of bitter gourd (*Momordica charantia*) peroxidase. Int. J. Biol. Macro, 41 56-63, ISSN: 0141-8130.

[89] Kvaratskhelia, M., Winkel, C. & Thorneley, R.N.F. (1997). Purification and characterization of a novel class III peroxidase isoenzyme from tea leaves. Plant Physiol, 114, 1237–1245, ISSN: 0032-0889.

[90] Tatarko, M. & Bumpus, J.A. (1997). Further studies on the inactivation by sodium azide of lignin peroxidase from Phanerochaete chrysosporium. Arch. Biochem. Biophys, 339, 200–209, ISSN: 0003-9861.

[91] Lorenzo, M., Moldes, D., Rodriguez, C.S. & Sanroma, M.A. (2005). Inhibition of laccase activity from Trametes versicolor by heavy metals and organic compounds. Chemosphere, 60, 1124–1128, ISSN: 0045-6535.

[92] Keyhani, J., Keyhani, E., Einollahi, N., Minai-Tehrani, D. & Zarchipour, S. (2003). Heterogeneous inhibition of horseradish peroxidase activity by cadmium. Biochim. Biophys. Acta, 1621, 140–148, ISSN: 0304-4165.

[93] Bagirova, N.A., Muginova, S.V., Shekhovtsova, T.N., Gazaryan, I.G. & Van Huystee, B. (2006). Effect of mercury (II) traces on catalytic activity of peanut and horseradish peroxidases. Anal. Lett. 39 521-1, ISSN: 0003-2719.

[94] vel Krawczyk, T.K., Moszczynska, M. & Trojanowicz, M. (2000). Inhibitive determination of mercury and other metal ions by potentiometric urea biosensor. Biosens. Bioelectron. 15, 681–691, ISSN: 0956-5663.

[95] Wang, J., Liang, Z., Wang, L., Fan, C. & Li, G. (2007). Electron transfer reactivity and catalytic activity of structurally rigidized haemoglobin. Sens. Act. B, 125, 17–21, ISSN: 0925-4005.

[96] Akhtar, S. & Husain, Q. (2006). Potential of immobilized bitter gourd (*Momordica charantia*) peroxidase in the removal of phenols from polluted water. Chemosphere, 65, 1228–1235, ISSN: 0045-6535.

[97] Alberti, B.N. & Klibanov, A.M. (1982). Peroxidase for removal of hazardous aromatics from industrial wastewaters. In: Exemer, J.H. (Ed.), In Detoxification of HazardousWastes. Ann Arbor Science Publishers, Ann Arbor, MI 349-256, ISSN:

[98] Jamal, F. & Goel, T. (2014). Diethylaminoethyl cellulose immobilized pointed gourd (*Trichosanthes dioica*) peroxidase in decolorization of synthetic dyes. J. Bioproces. Biotechniq, 4, 7, ISSN: 2155-9821.

[99] Jamal, F. & Singh, S. (2015). Application of diethylaminoethyl cellulose immobilized pointed gourd (*Trichosanthes dioica*) peroxidase in treatment of phenol and α-naphthol. J. Bioproces. Biotechniq, 5, 1, ISSN:2155-9821.

[100] Jamal, F., Pandey, P.K. & Qidwai, T. (2010). Potential of peroxidase enzyme from *Trichosanthes dioica* to mediate disperse dye decolorization in conjunction with redox mediators. J Mol Catal B: Enzy, 66, 177-181, ISSN: 0923-9820.

[101] Jamal, F., Qidwai, T., Pandey, P.K., Singh, R. & Singh, S. (2011). Azo and anthraquinone dye decolorization in relation to its molecular structure using soluble *Tricho-*

santhes dioica peroxidase supplemented with redox mediator. Catal. Commun, 12, 1218-1223, ISSN: 1566-7367.

[102] Jamal, F., Singh, S., Khatoon, S. & Mehrotra, S. (2013). Application of immobilized pointed gourd (*Trichosanthes dioica*) peroxidase concanavalin A complex on calcium alginate pectin gel in decolorization of synthetic dyes using batch processes and continuous two reactor system. J. Bioproces. Biotechniq, 3, 2, ISSN:2155-9821.

Chapter 3

Effect of Inorganic Additives in the Textile Dyes Removal by Ozonation

Abstract

Treatment of industrial wastewaters based on oxidative efficiency of ozone is still of great interest due to the high removal percentages of the initial pollutants and their by-products. In particular, the industrial dyes and their wastewaters have received special attention considering the large volumes of water produced daily with high concentration of chemical oxygen demand. In addition, the dyeing processes use some chemical additives to enhance the final quality of dyeing. The effect of all these additives on the wastewater treatment has been insufficiently explored. This chapter is focused on the study of different additives commonly used in dyeing process (Na_2SO_4 and Na_2CO_3 for Reactive Black 5 – RB5, Na_2SO_4 at different concentrations for Direct Red 28 – DR28, and acetic acid for Basic Green 4 – BG4) and their effect on ozonation efficiency in discoloration and dye decomposition. Moreover, the distribution of by-products obtained throughout the ozonation was compared when the additives are or not participating in the reaction. The influence of additives and dyes' chemical nature, their concentration, and the induced pH variation on dye solutions are explained using the results of ozone based on the treatment of the three dyes mentioned earlier. The characteristics of each dye combined with the corresponding additives over degradation and decomposition efficiency by ozone, and the by-product distribution was also studied.

Keywords: Dyes, discoloration, degradation, additives, ozonation

1. Introduction

1.1. Dyes and additives regularly used in textile industry

Dyes are colored unsaturated organic molecules that have strong affinity to natural and synthetic fabrics Kas131. Dyes are physically bound to the fiber by one or more physical forces, including hydrogen bonding, van der Waals, and ionic forces, and in certain cases chemically bound by covalent interaction Zol87.

Dyes are classified accordingly to different criteria such as color, intended use, trade name, chemical structure, and application Sar98, Per99. However, these last two options are the most widely used. Chemical structure indicates the chromophore groups in dyes, but it only designates basic structural aspects of them Teh10. This classification scheme and the major dye classes are detailed in Table 1.

Type of dye	Example of dye
Dyes containing anionic functional groups	Acid, direct, mordant, and reactive dyes
Dyes requiring chemical reaction before applications	Vat, azoic, and sulfur dyes
Dyes containing cationic groups	Basic dyes
Special colorant classes	Disperse, solvent, pigments, and natural dyes

Table 1. Classification of dyes and some examples

In this study, some examples of regular dyes were considered to prove the effect of ozone on discoloration and dye decomposition. Benzidine-based azo dyes (BBADs), such as Reactive Black 5 (RB5) and Direct Red 28 (DR28) are classical examples Kal07, Cho96, are the principal compounds in diverse industrial products and several secondary processes. BBADs correspond to about 20–30% of dyes used in the textile industry.

Dyes derived from triphenylmethane (TPM), which include Basic Red 9 (BR9), Basic Green 4 (BG4), and Basic Violet 3 (BV3), are largely used by textile industries in several dyeing practices. This collection of dyes is a primary matter in coloring plastics, gasoline, varnish, fats, oil, paper, leather, and waxes. BBA and TPM dyes are the most extended colorants used in industrial processes AnS02.

The improvement of the dyeing process requires some other chemical reagents known as auxiliaries or additives. These compounds increase the quality properties of the final product and improve the silkiness, texture, light resistance, stability, and so on. The surfactants, inorganic and organic salts, polymers, oligomers, and solubilities are compounds regularly used as additives, among others Zha04. Table 2 shows some examples of dyeing additives used in the textile industry considering the dye nature Gui.

Dye	Additive
Acid	Na_2SO_4, H_2SO_4, CH_2O_2, $C_2H_4O_2$, CH_3COONH_4, $(NH_4)_2SO_4$
Basic	CH_2O_2, $C_2H_4O_2$, $C_2H_2O_4$, $C_{76}H_{52}O_{46}$
Direct	$NaCl$, Na_2SO_4, $NaNO_2$, HCl
Reactive	$NaCl$, CON_2H_4, Na_2CO_3, P_2O_5, $Na_3P_2O_7$

Table 2. Additives used in the textile industry

1.2. Textile industry wastewater

Textile manufacturing processes consume considerable volumes of water. About 200–350 m^3 of wastewater per ton of finished products are regular volumes of textile industry where large amounts of dyes are used Pin04, Rob01. This particular type of wastewater is a complicated mixture of dyes, surfactants, inorganic and organic salts, polymers, oligomers, and stabilizing agents with other recalcitrant organics such as alcohols, aldehydes, and organic acids. All of these aforementioned compounds are used as additives in the dyeing, bleaching, scouring, and printing processes, except dyes Eco08.

Textile industry effluents contain high concentrations of toxic chemicals; high levels of biological oxygen demand (BOD, 110–5600 mg/L) and chemical oxygen demand (COD, 50–18,000 mg/L), a wide range of the pH values (2–14) and temperatures (15–70°C), a large quantity of total suspend solids (50–23,900 g/L), and a high degree of coloration Pal02, Raj06.

Despite the nature of dyes and their method of treatment, the decomposition of dyes produces different by-products that may be considered toxic to the human health and the aquatic life. BBADs have been identified as toxic compounds to aquatic life Khl10, and they are also considered as a possible source of a broad spectrum of immune suppression, respiratory, central nervous, and autoimmune diseases like leukemia, among others Wan02. The reaction of azo bonds of these dyes with different oxidants releases benzidine and other aromatic amines, which may cause adverse systemic health effects or even cancer Bey98. On the other hand, the TPM dye affects health, causing carcinogenesis, mutagenesis, teratogenesis, and respiratory infections Sha04.

2. Dyeing wastewater treatment

2.1. Regular methods of treatment for dyeing wastewater process

Dyeing wastewaters are usually treated using physical, biological, and chemical methods. In the last two decades, many results describing the physical treatment of these dyes have been presented. Adsorbents such as activated carbons, several industrial wastes, natural materials, bioadsorbents, and enhanced adsorption forces by ultrasound treatments have been described as remarkable examples of physical methods of treatment. The majority of dyes have high molecular weight and complex chemical structure. These characteristics yield to low biodegradability of dyeing wastewater due to the mixture toxicity of compounds. A few of the aforementioned results have proven that only complex bacterial consortium can decompose partially low concentrated dye solution (less than 50 mg/L).

To overcome the low efficiency of biological treatments, different chemical oxidation methods can be applied. In particular, the so-called advanced oxidation processes (AOPs) are effective to degrade dyes in water by the destruction of double bonds in molecules associated with chromophores Gog04, Koc02, Lia97, Maj97, Per03, Rob011, Wan03.

2.2. Ozonation of dyeing wastewater

Dye degradation by the ozone oxidative capacity may proceed in two mechanisms: direct (reaction between molecular ozone and dye) and indirect (based on chemical radicals produced by the interaction between ozone and hydroxyl ions) reactions. When pH is acid, molecular ozone selectively reacts with some specific sections of organic molecules such as double bonds or aromatic systems of reactive dyes in direct reaction. When pH is above 7.0, hydroxide radicals obtained by the reaction of ozone decomposition interact with many organic compounds Poz, Poz08.

Therefore, alkaline to neutral pH of dyeing wastewater motivates the unspecific radical reaction. However, the pH of the solution may decrease as a consequence of the formation of organic acids that are common final ozonation by-products. The reaction mechanism shifts toward the selective direct oxidation. Then, mixed mechanisms appear during the reaction despite the initial pH fixed in the reactor.

Conventional ozonation is an effective method to degrade rapidly these dyes in aqueous solutions (3–5 min, under the initial dye concentrations up to 50–150 mg/L) achieving a complete discoloration and degradation of the dye solution LiB07, Poz07. However, the formation of toxic by-products generated throughout the ozonation process must be a major issue when ozonation is proposed as the main treatment of textile industry wastewaters. The final compounds formed after ozonation are less toxic (simple organic acids), while the partial mineralization is confirmed by the decrease in the total organic carbon (TOC) and COD.

2.3. Additives in the dyeing industry: their effect on wastewater treatment

The presence of additives has not been considered in most of the chemical treatments of wastewaters produced by dyeing processes from different industries. These compounds can have different effects on treatment efficiency.

Indeed, their effect on the discoloration and decomposition dynamics of dyeing wastewater in ozonation can be very strong Fei07, Mut04. Nevertheless, the effect of additives has not been well studied.

The BBADs are usually added with inorganic salts in order to stabilize the mixture, but these compounds might generate some complexes with dyes. If some salts like carbonates are considered as additives, these inorganic salts appear as radicals' scavengers. Therefore, the presence of additives can change severely the ozonation kinetics by the concentration and nature of additives.

The aims of this study can be described as follows:

a. To study the effects of a textile additive such as Na_2SO_4 and Na_2CO_3 in the ozonation of two commercial BBADs (RB5 and DR28) and acetic acid (AA) in the degradation of BG4 by ozone.

b. To explain how additives accelerate or decelerate both the discoloration and the decomposition of studied dyes by a simple kinetic study of all systems.

c. To identify and characterize the final products formed in ozonation by high-performance liquid chromatography (HPLC).

3. Materials and methods

The experimental procedure was divided into four stages. The *first stage* was developed to study the interaction between ozone and additives without dyes. These experiments were used to understand the stoichiometric relationship between ozone and additives. In *the second stage*, the effect of three additives on the discoloration and the decomposition of three dyes during ozonation was studied. In *the third stage*, the reaction's by-products were previously identified using a simple spectrophotometric analysis. On the basis of the results obtained in these three stages, a kinetic study was performed to design a simplified reaction mechanism.

3.1. Preparation of dye solution

A set of synthetic textile dye solutions of DR28, RB5, and BG4 with concentrations of 50 and 150 mg/L dissolved in distilled water was prepared. The dyes, additives, and their concentrations to the ozonation process are summarized in Table 3.

The 50 mg/L solution was used to analyze discoloration kinetics, whereas the 150 mg/L concentration was used to identify the distribution of by-products and decomposition dynamics.

3.2. Ozonation procedure

Figure 1 shows the laboratory platform used to execute all the ozonation experiments. The temperature (23 ± 3°C) was fixed in a semi-batch reactor (batch for the liquid phase and continuous for the ozone) with a volume of 250 mL. An initial ozone concentration of 20 and 35 mg/L was selected to develop two sequences of experiments. Ozone concentrations were obtained using an ozone generator (discharge type), HTU500G ("AZCO" Industries Limited, Canada) with an oxygen flow of 0.5 L/min.

Dye concentration (50 and 150 mg/L)	**Additive**
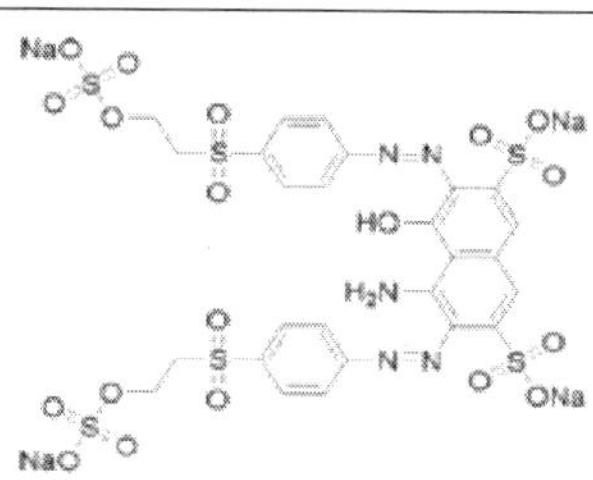 Reactive Black 5	Na_2SO_4 (30 g/L), Na_2CO_3 (100 g/L); individually and in mixture

Direct Red 28	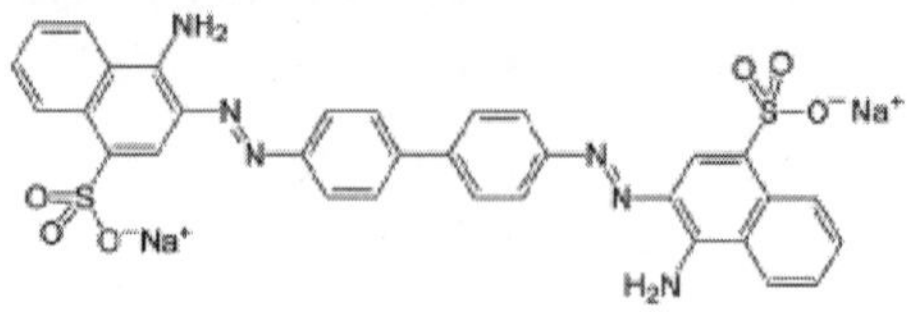	Na_2SO_4 (10, 40, and 80 g/L)
Basic Green 4	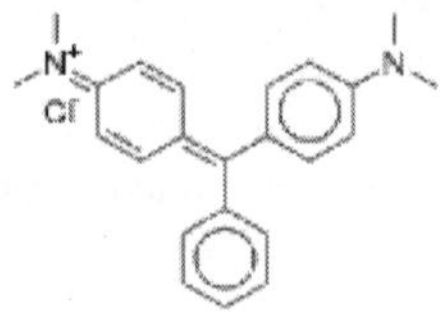	CH_3COOH 80% (3% v)

Table 3. Determination of dye systems and additives

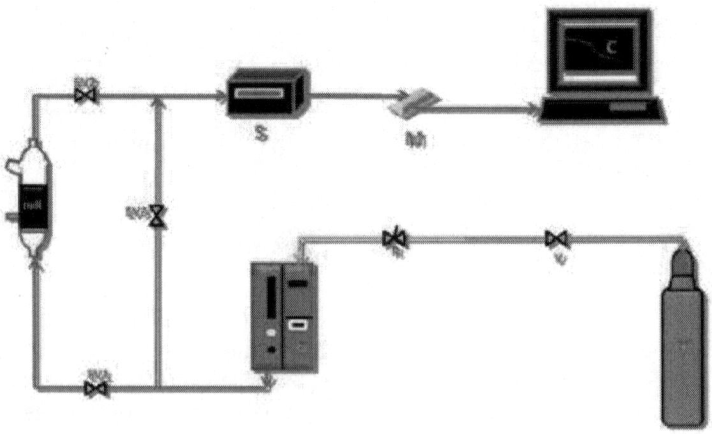

Figure 1. Experimental platform used to develop the ozonation: the oxygen tank (T), the ozone generator (G), the glass reactor (mR), the ozone sensor (S), the computer, the by-pass with solenoid valves (EV1, EV2, and EV3).

The ozone/oxygen mixture was distributed in the reactor using a porous ceramic diffuser located in the bottom section of the reactor. The ozone concentrations at the reactor's inlet and outlet gas streams were measured using an ozone analyzer model BMT-930, which was connected to a personal computer. Data acquisition software was used to obtain the current ozone concentration.

3.3. Analytical methods

Along the oxidation process, samples were taken at different times, which were analyzed by UV–Vis Spectrophotometer (Lambda 2B, Perkin Elmer). These samples were analyzed to obtain the discoloration dynamics (under dye concentration of 50 mg/L) by UV–vis spectrum variation at 343 nm for DR28, 311 nm for RB5, and 250 nm for BG4. The pH variation throughout the ozonation was measured using a potentiometer (Portable pH/CON 10 and Waterproof pH/CON 10 meter, OAKTON).

The identification of by-products was performed by a HPLC analysis, (Perkin Elmer) equipped with UV–vis detector series 200 (190–360 nm) with a dye concentration of 150 ppm and an ozone concentration of 30 ppm. To obtain the dye degradation dynamics, a Platinum C18100A column (PerkinElmer, Inc.; 25034.6 mm) was used for three dyes. The mobile phase was acetonitrile–water (95:5) at 311 nm for RB5, acetonitrile–water–methanol (50:5:45) at 343 nm for DR28, and acetonitrile–water (2:98) at 250 nm for BG4. To identify the intermediates (formation and decomposition), a Spherisorb Silica column (25034.6 mm; Alltech, Nicholasville, Kentucky) was used at 255 nm. In this instance, the mobile phase was acetonitrile–water (80:20). In the case of the BG4 ozonation, the final products were identified using a column of prevail organic acid (150 × 4.6 mm, Alltech). The mobile phase was monobasic potassium phosphate 2.25 mM at pH 2.5 (for dye without additives at 211 nm) and 3.6 mM for analyzing the solution of dye complemented with AA. The HPLC analysis for all samples was performed using a sample volume of 30 μL, and the carrier flow was fixed to 0.8 mL/min.

4. Results and discussion

4.1. Additive ozonation

In order to interpret correctly, the possible interactions between the ozone dye and the ozone additive are necessary to study in each system separately. The concentrations of all additives correspond to those used in the textile industry. Table 4 shows the ozone consumption and characteristic pH to each additive solution.

Additive	Concentration (g/L)	Ozone consume (mole)	pH
Water	–	0.0075	5.6
Na_2CO_3	30	0.0263	12.4
Na_2SO_4	100	0.0067	7.8
Na_2CO_3/Na_2SO_4	30/100	0.0305	12.7
Na_2SO_4	10	0.0076	7.8
Na_2SO_4	40	0.0068	6.5
Na_2SO_4	80	0.0066	6.3
CH_3COOH (80%)	3% $_V$	0.0082	1.52

Table 4. Characteristics of additive solutions

The pH of the additive solutions has different values depending on the nature of the additive. In general, the Na_2SO_4 solutions have shown neutral pH (6.3–7.8), the Na_2CO_3 solutions have shown basic pH (12.4), and the AA solution has shown acidic pH (1.52). The solution of the additive mixture (Na_2CO_3/Na_2SO_4) has basic pH due to the influence of the Na_2CO_3 presence.

Figure 2 shows the ozonograms of the four additive solutions in comparison with the ozone saturation in distilled water as reference. The Na_2SO_4 and the AA did not show any interaction with ozone. On the other hand, the ozonograms of the Na_2CO_3 and the salt mixture (Na_2CO_3/Na_2SO_4) solution are different to the reference with a final concentration smaller than the one used at the reactor's input. This confirms the partial ozone decomposition (about 30%) to other oxidative species.

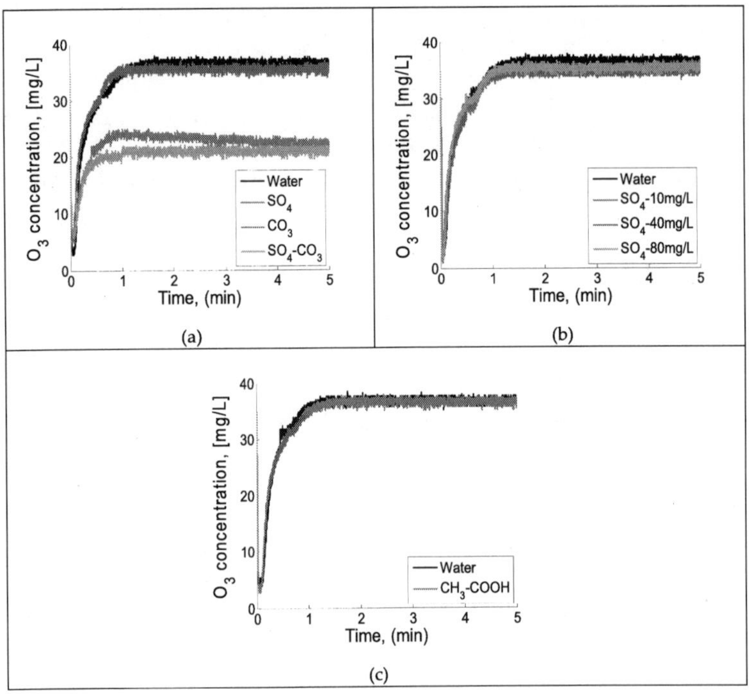

Figure 2. Ozonograms of the additives: (a) Na_2CO_3 and Na_2CO_3/Na_2SO_4, (b) Na_2SO_4 at different concentrations, and (c) CH_3COOH.

When the pH of the solution is above 7.0, the ozone decomposition promotes the formation of hydroxyl radicals. The hydroxyl radicals interacted with the carbonate ion (CO_3^{2-}), following the well-known scheme to form the carbonate ion radical ($CO_3^{\bullet -}$) that did not react with ozone but can react with dye and constitute another method of oxidation Bel05.

The difference between distilled water and sulfate solutions of ozone consumption was practically undetectable. This condition could be a consequence of the poor sulfate ions reaction with the ozone at that detected pH interval. A similar behavior was determined for the AA solution because there is no ozone consumption. Furthermore, those kinds of compounds have lower reaction kinetic constant with ozone (10^{-3} to 10^{-1}).

4.2. Additive effect on ozonation dynamics of dyes

In general, the main parameter used to characterize the treatment efficiency of the textile wastewaters is the presence of the color and the discoloration degree. However, the removal of color does not mean that the dye was completely decomposed during the same time. In the present investigation, dye decomposition was also studied and compared with the dynamics of the color elimination by HPLC. In this case, the initial colorant concentration was 150 mg/L. To evaluate the effect of the additives on their discoloration and decomposition dynamics, the dye solutions with and without additives were ozonated at the same operation conditions. By the determination of the stoichiometry of the reaction with ozone, it is possible to propose the scheme of the decomposition mechanisms. These experiments were executed to evaluate the ozone consumption by the dye and the interactions with the additive.

Table 5 shows the stoichiometric results obtained during dye ozonation with and without additives. This relationship was determined using the total ozone consumed during the reaction and the total moles of dye. This ratio is usually called the ozone dose.

In case of RB5 added with sulfate decreased the amount of ozone consumed per mole of dye. The formation of peroxysulfate radicals can be the cause to produce this decrement. One must recall that only a portion of ozonogram is used to perform the ozone dose determination that corresponds to the expected kinetic behavior of the decomposition of the initial dye. When carbonate was the only additive for RB5, the ozone dose increased almost 20% that confirms the scavenger nature of this salts in the ozonation of dyes. Moreover, when both additives (sulfate and carbonate) were in the reaction, the ozone dose increased 33%. So, a synergic effect occurred between both additives and ozone, yielding to consume more ozone in this case.

System	Concentration (g/L)	Ozone dose (mole O_3/mole dye)
RB5	–	3.966
RB5 – Na_2SO_4	30	3.465
RB5 – $CaCO_3$	100	4.753
RB5 – Na_2SO_4 – $CaCO_3$	30/100	5.297
DR28	–	3.432
DR28 – Na_2SO_4 (10 g/L)	10	6.165
DR28 – Na_2SO_4 (40 g/L)	40	5.194
DR28 – Na_2SO_4 (80 g/L)	80	4.594
BG4	–	2.701
BG4 – CH_3COOH	3% $_V$	3.629

Table 5. Stoichiometric ratio of ozone consumed during dye decomposition

When the DR28 dye was evaluated, the ozone doses in systems with sulfate showed an inverse relation with the additive concentration. This means that 80 mg/L of ozone consumption was 74% smaller than the result obtained when the additive concentration was fixed at 10 mg/L. Nevertheless, despite the additive concentration, the ozone dose was higher than the case when there was no additive in the reaction. The BG4 ozonation is carried out in the presence of AA as additive; it was shown that the acid presence has a significant effect on the ozone consumption being 34% higher than the additive and dye solutions, this may be by the interactions between the additive and the dye generating some kind of chemical complexes.

As a preliminary conclusion, the presence of additives increased ozone consumption because the ozone decomposes itself to another compound as hydroxyl radicals or reacts with the ions from the additives to generate new oxidative species.

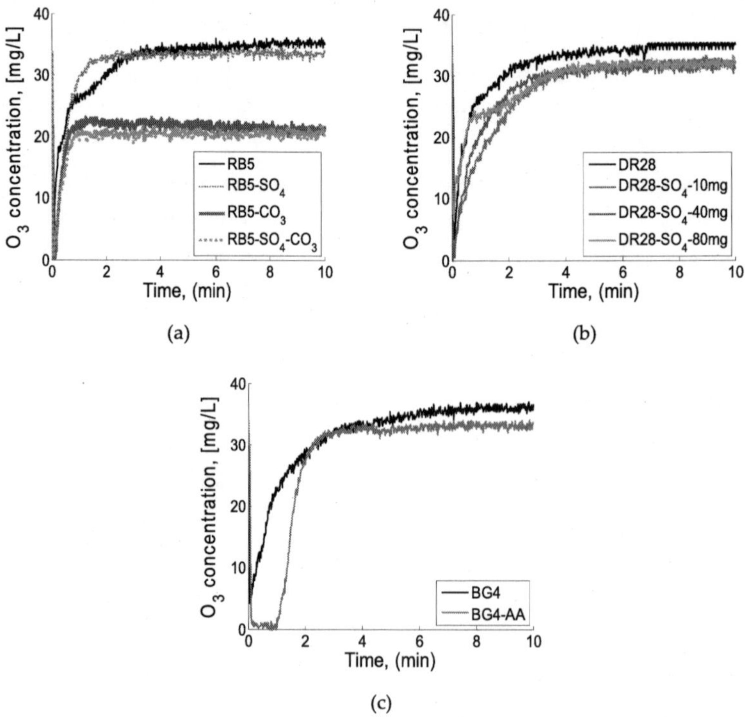

Figure 3. Discoloration dynamics of the three dyes with and without additives

4.3. Effect of additives on pH variation

Different studies Poz07,Fei07 have proven that pH decreases along the ozonation. This fact has been explained considering that initial molecule decomposition yields to organic acid such as oxalic, formic, maleic, and so on, which triggers the acid pH. Table 6 shows the pH variation of all ozonation with and without additives.

In particular, when additives were in the reactor and the initial pH was basic, the final pH of solutions remained alkaline. This is a remarkable consequence of additives that brings a basic pH, while the concentration of organic acids generated in the ozonation reaction is not enough to force the decrement of this parameter. So, the buffer capacity promoted by additives (in the case of inorganic salts) modifies the reaction mechanism. Moreover, the null variation of pH observed when carbonate was in the reactor can obey a different process where carbonate served as scavenger of free radicals. Finally, when AA was considered as additive, pH did not vary because initial pH was already strongly acid (2.8). The poor variation of pH can be a consequence of the different pK_a of all other organic acids that are higher than the pH fixed at the beginning of the reaction.

Dye	pH initial	pH final
RB5	5.5	3
RB5 – Na^2SO^4	7	9.5
RB5 – $CaCO^3$	11	11
RB5 – Na_2SO_4 – $CaCO_3$	11	11
DR28	7.8	4
DR28 – Na_2SO_4 (10 g/L)	11	11
DR28 – Na_2SO_4 (40 g/L)	7.8	4
DR28 – Na_2SO_4 (80 g/L)	7.8	4
BG4	4	3
BG4 – CH_3COOH	2.8	3

Table 6. Average variation of pH determined in ozonation experiments with and without additives

4.4. Additive effect on dye solution discoloration and decomposition dynamics by ozone oxidative activity

4.4.1. Discoloration dynamics

According some researchers Zha04,Wan03,LiB07, the first stage in ozone reaction with dye is the attack to the chromophore groups that give the color properties to the molecule.

In order to follow the presence of chromophore groups through ozonation process, the UV–vis spectroscopy was used at each dye's characteristic wavelength: 311 nm for RB5, 343 nm for DR28, and 250 nm for BG4. Table 7 contains the information of the total time discoloration for each ozonation system when the dye initial concentration was 50 mg/L.

In case of RB5, the discoloration process was faster when the mixture of additives participated in the ozonation. The total discoloration time was reduced about 90% when compared with the case with no additives. This percentage decreased to 82.5% when only the carbonate was used as additive.

Treatment system	Discoloration time (min)	Discoloration (k, L/mol s)	Decomposition time	Decomposition (k, L/mol s)
NR5	4.0	3.51×10^4	5.0	0.0335×10^4
NR5 – Na_2CO_3	0.75	0.140×10^4	3.0	0.0858×10^4
NR5 – Na_2SO_4	0.75	0.502×10^4	0.75	0.176×10^4
NR5 – Na_2SO_4/Na_2CO_3	0.5	42.9×10^4	6.0	0.0682×10^4
RD28	3.0	5.68×10^4	15	0.0201×10^4
RD28 – Na_2SO_4 (10 g/L)	1.0	1.07×10^4	6.0	0.0987×10^4
RD28 – Na_2SO_4 (40 g/L)	4.0	1.70×10^4	6.0	0.0897×10^4
RD28 – Na_2SO_4 (80 g/L)	5.0	0.63×10^4	6.0	0.0395×10^4
VB4	2.0	3.02×10^4	1.0	0.0813×10^4
VB4 – CH_3COOH	1.0	9.6×10^4	15	1.37×10^4

Table 7. Summary of discoloration and decomposition dynamics including reaction periods of time as well as the pseudo-monomolecular kinetic reaction rate constants

If sulfate was the additive to the dye solution, the percentage reduction of discoloration time was equal (82.5%). This can be explained considering that some by-products such as hydroquinone or catechol bring some kind of coloration to the solution.

In the case of DR28 ozonation without additives, the discoloration was observed after 3 min of the reaction; however, when sulfate was added with a concentration of 10 gm/L, this time decreased more than 65%.

When the additive concentration increased, the discoloration times also increased. This condition can be a consequence of the solution pH that was fixed to 11.0 and that may yield to increase in the hydroxyl radicals' formation, which in turn promotes the peroxysulfate radical (2.01 V) development accelerating dye solution discoloration. The formation of mechanisms was explained in reference.

At alkaline pH, the ozone decomposes itself to hydroxyl radicals, which can react with sulfate ions, originating the peroxysulphate ions which due to its oxidative nature (2.01 V) attacks the dye molecule in different positions resulting in its faster fragmentation [32].

The AA does not represent a significant effect on discoloration time because in both systems the same efficacy (95%) was observed in the first minute.

Some reaction mechanisms described a feasible reaction scheme of RR22 decomposition when the peroxysulfate radical appears in the reactor [39]. According to this scheme, there are two possible stages when the dye can be decomposed. The first considers the interaction with the chromophore group where possible links may be formed by the interactions of additives or ions. The second one involves the complete molecule decomposition generating some by-products and finally some short-chain acids. In ozonation, this scheme confirms that the complete reaction did not yield to complete mineralization.

4.4.2. Decomposition time

Actually, the main parameter used to characterize the efficacy of wastewater treatment from the dyeing process is the discoloration time; however, this does not mean that total dye decomposition may occur at that stage. So, it is necessary to study this part of the reaction in order to characterize the total time decomposition with and without the additive presence.

Table 6 also presents the total decomposition time, where it has been proved that the additive presence has a strong effect on this parameter depending on the additive and the dye under analysis. A set of HPLC studies were carried out to study the decomposition of the dye molecule. These analyses were executed considering an initial dye concentration of 15 mg/L.

When the ozonation of RB5 without additives was evaluated, a decomposition efficiency of 90% was reached after 5 min of reaction. When additives participated in the reaction (individually), this efficiency was reached before 1 min of the reaction and 3 min when the corresponding additives were mixed. This time decreased when additives were in the reactor due to the presence of diverse oxidative ions that accelerated dye molecule decomposition. The same effect was observed in the case of DR28 dye where the decomposition time decreased from 15 min to 6 min. At that reaction time, a 60% of decomposition in the first reaction minute was observed.

If the BG4 dye was ozonation, the presence of the AA increased in the degradation time. Under these conditions, 90% of degradation after 15 min of the reaction was achieved when compared with the dye without additive where the same efficiency was reached before 1 min of reaction.

Discoloration and decomposition times were reduced under the presence of additives enhancing the respective efficiencies in the cases of RB5 and DR28 systems. However, BG4 does not have the same behavior.

4.5. Discoloration and decomposition kinetics

According to some researchers WYu06, Lop07,HSh06, WZh06, MSL07, the study of reaction kinetics was made based on discoloration dynamics, using an equation of pseudo-first order. The following equation was used to determine the reaction kinetic constant.

The model used to characterize either discoloration or decomposition during the dye ozonation has the mathematical structure given by:

$$\frac{dDye(t)}{dt} = -k_r Dye(t) O_3(t), \tag{1}$$

where k_r, the reaction rate, is constant associated to the viscosity changes, $Dye(t)$ is the variation of either discoloration or decomposition during ozonation, and $O_3(t)$ is the calculated dissolved ozone concentration measured indirectly by the ozonogram.

The model described by Equation (1) is linear with respect to their corresponding parameters. However, the model has as an independent variable the time derivative of the variable under modeling analysis. This situation complicates the parametric characterization of the reaction proposed to model the effect of ozone on these two variables.

The solution of the parametric identification problem that is to get k_r can be obtained by the application of a robust exact differentiator. This differentiator can be implemented by the super-twisting algorithm. So, consider that the signal $f(t)$ to be differentiated satisfies $|f(t)| < f^+, \forall t > 0$. Hence, the super-twisting algorithm obeys the following structure:

$$\begin{aligned} \dot{z}_1(t) = v(t) = z_2(t) - \lambda_1 \left|z_1(t) - f(t)\right|^{1/2} \mathbf{sign}\left(z_1(t) - f(t)\right) \\ \dot{z}_2(t) = -\lambda_2 \mathbf{sign}\left(z_1(t) - f(t)\right) \end{aligned} \tag{2}$$

A sufficient condition to recover the differentiation of function $f(t)$ is to select λ_1, $\lambda_2 > 0$. As an example, under the condition proposed to the gains, the model presented in Equation (1) can be represented as follows:

$$y(t) = -k_r x(t) O_3(t) + \varepsilon(t), \tag{3}$$

where the variable $y(t)$ is the approximation of the time derivative of the variable under analysis. The term $\varepsilon(t)$ describes the approximation error produced by the implementation of the differentiator.

The parametric identification problem presented in Equation (3) can be solved by the well-known least mean square method. This method cannot be applied directly because the signals of $x(t)$ and $O_3(t)$ are measured with different sampling times. Therefore, an interpolation algorithm was applied to homogenize the number of samples that can be used in the parametric identification method. The interpolation algorithm used an approximation based on third-order polynomials (cubic). The interpolation algorithm used the interpolation based on ozonogram. The same algorithm was applied to characterize both the double-bond dynamics and the color or dye concentration variation. The constants obtained by this method were summarized in Table 7.

4.6. By-product distribution in dye wastewater treated by ozone with and without additives

Several studies have reported that the final compounds formed by the reaction between dyes and ozone, which are short-chain organic acids, without reaching full mineralization due to those compounds have low reactivity with the ozone.

Table 8 shows the final compounds identified by the HPLC technique and their respective concentrations. Oxalic, formic, fumaric, and maleic acids where the principal compounds identified being oxalic acid that has a higher accumulation (40–120 mg/L).

System	By-product	Concentration (mg/L)
RB5	Oxalic acid	4
	Formic acid	50
RB5 – Na_2SO_4	Oxalic acid	50
	Maleic acid	Traces
RB5 – Na_2CO_3	Maleic acid	Traces
	Fumaric acid	Traces
	Oxalic acid	100
RB5 – Na_2SO_4 – Na_2CO_3	Maleic acid	Traces
	Fumaric acid	Traces
	Oxalic acid	Traces
DR28	Fumaric acid	Traces
	Maleic acid	Traces
	Oxalic acid	10
	Formic acid	40
DR28 – Na_2SO_4 (10 g/L)	Oxalic acid	120
DR28 – Na_2SO_4 (40 g/L)	Oxalic acid	80
DR28 – Na_2SO_4 (80 g/L)	Oxalic acid	50
BG4	Maleic acid	Traces
	Oxalic acid	18
	Formic acid	20
BG4 – CH_3COOH	Maleic acid	Traces
	Oxalic acid	50
	Formic acid	Traces

Table 8. Composition and the concentrations of main products formed in ozonation

So, in the case of DR28 ozonation, the fumaric (traces), maleic (traces), oxalic (10 mg/L), and formic (40 mg/L) acids were identified. The presence of the last acid attributes to the partial decomposition of oxalic acid. However, in the presence of additives, only oxalic acid was formed (50–120 mg/L), and its concentration was inversely proportional to the sodium sulfate concentration. In addition, the additive has a significant effect on the formation dynamics of the acid.

When RB5 was ozonated, the concentrations of organic acids changed in the presence of additives. So, without additives, 50 mg/L of formic acids and 4 mg/L of oxalic acid were detected. With sodium carbonate, the content of oxalic acid increased up to 100 mg/L, and in the presence of sodium sulfate, the oxalic acid concentration was 80 mg/L. In the system with the salt mixture, practically, organic acids are not observed (traces). This fact is attributed to the summary effect of the hydroxyl and sulfate radicals, and the peroxysulfate ions formed, which provokes, practically, the complete mineralization of acids.

During BG4 ozonation, several organic acids were generated, such as maleic, oxalic, and formic acids (0.3, 18.0, and 20.0 mg/L, respectively). In the presence of AA, the oxalic acid concentration was increased to 50 ppm. In particular, the AA has a significant effect on acid accumulation. This effect is negative.

5. Conclusions

Ozonation is an efficient process for the treatment of textile wastewater that has been proven through the studies of discoloration and decomposition of RB5, RD28, and BG4 without and with salt and organic acid additives.

The effect of additives on ozonation dynamics of salts and acids without dye could be observed because of OH8 formed by the ozone decomposition reaction. These radicals likely react with salt ions of additives (and) with the formation of some reactive species that serve as oxidizing agents in the reaction. In the presence of additives, pH was modified (for the systems of RB5/ Na_2SO_4, Na_2CO_3, and RB5/Na_2CO_3), and the sodium carbonate effect was strong. AA did not react with ozone, but it increased the discoloration and the decomposition initial rates of BG4. This was confirmed by the comparison of the values of the reaction rate constants with and without additives.

Maleic, oxalic, and formic acids were formed in dye ozonation, and the presence of the additive increased their concentration except for formic acid.

Actually, the pH remained constant through the reaction. Carbonate stabilizes pH, and, very probably, it serves as a buffer. The presence of additives increases the discoloration and the decomposition rate of dyes studied. This was confirmed by comparing the values of the reaction rate constants with and without additives. In dye ozonation, fumaric, maleic, oxalic, and formic acids were formed, and the presence of additives increased their concentration in all systems studied. A plausible and possible mechanism for each dye was proposed based on the results achieved in this study and those reported in different preliminary studies.

References

[1] M. B. Kasiri, N. Modirshahla and H. Mansouri, "Decolorization of organic dye solution by ozonation: Optimization with response surface methodology," *International Journal of Industrial Chemistry*, vol. 4, no. 3, pp. 1–10, 2013.

[2] G. Zollinger, Color chemistry: Syntheses, properties and applications of organic dyes and pigments, Zurich: Wiley-VCH, 1987.

[3] J. Sarasa, M. P. Roche, M. P. Ormad, E. Gimeno, A. Puig and J. L. Ovelleiro, "Treatment of a wastewater resulting from dyes manufacturing with ozone and chemical coagulation," *Water Research*, vol. 32, no. 9, pp. 2721–2727, 1998.

[4] P. Peralta-Zamora, A. Kunz, S. G. de Moraes, R. Pelegrini, P. de Campos Moleiro, J. Reyes and N. Duran, "Degradation of reactive dyes I. A comparative study of ozonation, enzymatic and photochemical processes," *Chemosphere*, vol. 38, no. 4, pp. 835–852, 1999.

[5] A. R. Tehrani-Bagha, N. M. Mahmoodi and F. M. Menger, "Degradation of a persistent organic dye from colored textile wastewater by ozonation," *Desalination*, vol. 260, no. 1, pp. 34–38, 2010.

[6] S. D. Kalme, G. K. Parshetti, S. U. Jadhav and S. P. Govindwar, "Biodegradation of benzidine based dye direct blue-6 by Pseudomonas desmolyticum NCIM 2112," *Bioresource technology*, vol. 98, no. 7, pp. 1405–1410, 2007.

[7] G. Choudhary, "Human health perspectives on environmental exposure to benzidine: A review," *Chemosphere*, vol. 32, no. 2, pp. 267–291, 1996.

[8] S. Y. An, S. K. Min, I. H. Cha, Y. L. Choi, Y. S. Cho, C. H. Kim and Y. C. Lee, "Decolorization of triphenylmethane and azo dyes by *Citrobacter* sp.," *Biotechnology Letters*, vol. 24, no. 12, pp. 1037–1040, 2002.

[9] F. Zhang, A. Yediler, X. Liang and A. Kettrup, "Effects of dye additives on the ozonation process and oxidation by-products: A comparative study using hydrolyzed CI Reactive Red 120," *Dyes and Pigments*, vol. 60, no. 1, pp. 1–7, 2004.

[10] C. Hessel, C. Allegre, M. Maisseu, F. Charbit and P. Moulin, "Guidelines and legislation for dye house effluents," *Enviromental Management*, vol. 83, pp. 171–180, 2007.

[11] H. M. Pinheiro, E. Touraud and O. Thomas, "Aromatic amines from azo dye reduction: Status review with emphasis on direct UV spectrophotometric detection in textile industry wastewaters," *Dyes and Pigments*, vol. 61, no. 2, pp. 121–139, 2004.

[12] T. Robinson, G. McMullan, R. Marchant and P. Nigam, "Remediation of dyes in textile effluent: A critical review on current treatment technologies with a proposed alternative," *Bioresource Technology*, vol. 77, no. 3, pp. 247–255, 2001.

[13] "Eco-friendly reactive dyes for dyeing and printing industry," *Dyestuffs and Colouration*, vol. 3, 2008.

[14] A. Pala and E. Tokat, "Color removal from cotton textile industry wastewater in an activated sludge system with various additives," *Water Research*, vol. 36, no. 11, pp. 2920–2925, 2002.

[15] D. Rajkumar and J. G. Kim, "Oxidation of various reactive dyes with in situ electro-generated active chlorine for textile dyeing industry wastewater treatment," *Journal of Hazardous Materials*, vol. 136, no. 2, pp. 203–212, 2006.

[16] R. Khlifi, L. Belbahri, S. Woodward, M. Ellouz, A. Dhouib, S. Sayadi and T. Mechichi, "Decolourization and detoxification of textile industry wastewater by the laccase-mediator system," *Journal of Hazardous Materials*, vol. 175, no. 1, pp. 802–808, 2010.

[17] C. Wang, A. Yediler, D. M. Lienert, Z. Wang and A. Kettrup, "Toxicity evaluation of reactive dyestuffs, auxiliaries and selected effluents in textile finishing industry to luminescent bacteria *Vibrio fischeri*," *Chemosphere*, vol. 46, no. 2, pp. 339–344, 2002.

[18] M. I. Beydilli, S. G. Pavlostathis and W. C. Tincher, "Decolorization and toxicity screening of selected reactive azo dyes under methanogenic conditions," *Water Science and Technology*, vol. 38, no. 4, pp. 225–232, 1998.

[19] D. K. Sharma, H. S. Saini, M. Singh, S. S. Chimni and B. S. Chadha, "Isolation and characterization of microorganisms capable of decolorizing various triphenylmethane dyes," *Journal of Basic Microbiology*, vol. 44, no. 1, pp. 56–65, 2004.

[20] P. R. Gogate and A. B. Pandit, "A review of imperative technologies," *Advanced Environment Research*, vol. 8, pp. 553–597, 2004.

[21] M. Koch, A. Yediler, D. Lienert, G. Insel and A. Kettrup, "Ozonation of hydrolyzed azo dye reactiveyellow 84," *Chemosphere*, vol. 46, no. 1, pp. 109–113, 2002.

[22] S. Liakou, S. Pavlou and G. Lyberatos, "Ozonation of azo dyes," *Water Science Technology*, vol. 35, pp. 279–286, 1997.

[23] A. S. Majcen, T. Slokar and T. Taufer, "Decloration of chlorotriazine reactive azo dyes with H2O2/UV," *Dyes and Pigments*, vol. 33, no. 4, pp. 281–298, 1997.

[24] J. K. Perkowski and L. Kos, "Decolouration of model dye house wastewater with advanced oxidation process," *Fibres and Textiles in Eastern Europe*, vol. 11, pp. 67–71, 2003.

[25] T. Robinson, G. McMullan, R. Marchant and P. Nigam, "Remediation of dyes in textile effluent: A critical review on current treatment technologies with proposed alternatives," *Bioresource Technology*, vol. 77, pp. 247–255, 2001.

[26] C. Wang, A. Yediler, D. Lienert, Z. Wang and A. Kettrup, "Ozonation of an azo dye C.I. Remazol Black 5 and toxicological assessment of its oxidation products," *Chemosphere*, vol. 52, pp. 1225–1232, 2003.

[27] T. Poznyak and I. Chairez, "Kinetic study of toxic pollutants decomposition by ozone in landfill leachate using a numerical adaptive method," *International Journal of Environmental Engineering. Special Issue in Progress in Landfill Management and Landfill Emission Reduction*, vol. 3, no. 3–4, pp. 221–239, 2011.

[28] T. Poznyak, G. L. Bautista, I. Chairez, R. I. Cordova and E. Rios, "Decomposition of toxic pollutants in landfill leachate by ozone after coagulation treatment," *Journal of Hazardous Materials*, vol. 152, no. 3, pp. 1108–1114, 2008.

[29] C. Li-Bing, X. H. Xing, A. F. Yu, Y. N. Zhou, X. L. Sun and B. Jurick, "Enhanced ozonation of simulated dye stuff wastewater by micro bubbles," *Chemosphere*, vol. 37, pp. 1854–1860, 2007.

[30] T. Poznyak, P. Conlindres and I. Chairez, "Treatment of textile industrial dyes by simple ozonation with water recirculation," *Journal of Mexican Chemical Society*, vol. 51, no. 2, pp. 81–86, 2007.

[31] Z. Feifang, A. Yediler and X. Liang, "Decomposition pathways and reaction intermediate formation of the purified hydrolyzed azo reactive dye C.I. Reactive Red 120 during ozonation," *Chemosphere*, vol. 67, pp. 712–717, 2007.

[32] M. S. Muthukumar, D. Sargunamari, M. Senthilkumar and N. Selvakumar, "Studies on the effect of inorganic salts on decolouration of acid dye effluents by ozonation," *Dyes and Pigments*, vol. 64, pp. 221–228, 2004.

[33] J. F. Beltrán, Ozone reactions kinetics for water and wastewater systems, Boca Raton, Florida: Lewis Publishers, 2005.

[34] W. Yu and K. Young, "Photocatalytic degradation of RR22 in aqueous solution by UV-LED radiation," *Water Research*, vol. 40, pp. 2249–2258, 2006.

[35] A. Lopez-Lopez, J.-S. Pic and H. Debellefontaine, "Ozonation of azo dye in a semi-batch reactor: A determination of the molecular and radical contribution," *Chemosphere*, vol. 66, pp. 2120–2126, 2007.

[36] H. Shu, " Degradation of dyehouse effluent containing C.I. Direct Blue 199 by processes of ozonation, UV/H2O2 and in sequence of ozonation with UV/H2O2," *Journal of Hazardous Materials*, vol. B133, pp. 92–98, 2006.

[37] W. Zhao, Z. Wu and D. Wang, "Ozone direct oxidation kinetics of cationic red X-GRL in aqueous solution," *Journal of Hazardous Materials*, vol. B137, pp. 1859–1865, 2006.

[38] M. S. Lucas, A. A. Dias, A. Sampaio, C. Amaral and J. A. Peres, "Degradation of a textile reactive azo dye by a combined chemical – biological process: Fenton's reagent –yeast," *Water Research*, vol. 41, pp. 1103–1109, 2007.

[39] W. Yu Wang, Young Ku. Photocatalytic degradation of RR22 in aqueous solution by UV-LED radiation. Water Research. 40(2006)2249-2258

Chapter 4

Bioremediation and Detoxification Technology for Treatment of Dye(s) from Textile Effluent

Abstract

The aim of this chapter is to demonstrate the technical and economic feasibility of an integrated process for microbial treatment of dye(s) containing wastewater from textile effluent that evaluates the efficiency and effectiveness to meet the dye(s)' maximum contaminant level. This chapter covers the whole process of microbial treatment methods that are adopted for dye removal to make an eco-friendly system. The purpose of this treatment technology includes process modifications and engineering approaches. It comprises existing technologies with new advancement technology at all stages of the process. This chapter evaluates the reliability of technologies for small and large systems to make the system cost-effective. It also demonstrates how genetically engineered micro-organism works and shows that the "microbial treatment platform for dye removal" can operate with positive economical balance to economize the bioprocess technology. Thus, future prospects of microbial treatment technology should be directed not only how to economically improve bioremediation but also how to effectively commercialize such economically sounded "bio-based" treatment methods in different industries.

Keywords: Dye(s), color, bioremediation, technology, genetic engineering

1. Introduction

The increasing demand for rapid urbanization, changing consumption, population growth, and fast socioeconomic development has inevitably led to an increased water pollution on the biosphere, which leads to environment pollution [1]. The effluents generated from domestic and industrial activities constitute the major sources of the natural water pollution load such as dye(s), heavy metal, cyanide, toxic organics, nitrogen, phosphorous, phenols, suspended solids, color, and turbidity. This pollution load is a great obligation in terms of wastewater management, which not only increases treatment cost considerably but also introduces a wide range of chemical pollutants and microbial contaminants to water sources. Dye(s) and pigments used in textile industries are playing a crucial role in value addition, appearance, and fulfillment of customers' desire. It has been found that the use of synthetic dye(s) has been rapidly increased in textile industries due to cost-effectiveness in synthesis and high stability. In addition, various colors can be synthesized when compared to natural dye(s). In consequences, a huge discharge of polluted effluent was found in different industries. It has been reported that color can be visible at a concentration higher than 1 mg/L [2,3]. It is obvious that the dye(s) containing water interferes with penetration of sunlight, which retards photosynthesis. In addition, it also inhibits the growth of aquatic flora and fauna by interfering with gas solubility [4]. In addition, it was experimented that there are so many dyes that are carcinogenic in nature [5]. As the use of synthetic dye(s) has tremendously increased in the industrial process and humans are being exposed to them more, water pollution due to these dyes is a critical issue in terms of human health concerns and serious ecological consequences. Hence, there is an urgent need for removal of these dyes from the effluents.

There are several methods applied for the removal of these dyes from wastewater, which include physical, chemical, and biological. However, these technologies vary in terms of their efficiency, cost, and environmental impact. Hence, there is an urgent need for all researchers to find out an efficient, inexpensive, and environmentally friendly system to reduce dye content in wastewater at acceptable levels.

2. Background to dye(s)

Colorants are chemicals that give color to the materials to which they are applied. Colorants can be classified into pigments and dye(s), and the pigments and dye(s) mainly differ from each other based on their solubility. Pigments retain their crystalline or particulate nature during the application. They are always combined in some medium that is applied to a surface. On the other hand, dyes are soluble and diffuse into the material and become an integral part. The former are usually used in paints, inks, and polymers, and the latter are applied not only mainly to textiles but also to paper, leather, food, and other products. For a colored substance to be regarded as a useful dyestuff, factors beyond solubility are required. A dyestuff must be substantive for a textile and thus be preferentially taken up by the fiber, usually from an aqueous solution [6].

3. The physical basis of color

Dyes possess color due to the absorbance of light in the range of 400–700 nm, i.e., in the visible spectrum; a dye possesses at least one chromophore (color-possessing group); it should have a conjugated system such as structure with alternate double bonds and single bonds. The dye molecule exhibits resonance of electrons, which is a stabilizing force in organic compounds [7]. When among these properties if anyone is not present, then the molecular structure of color will be lost (dye chemistry). Chromophore undergoes π–π^* and n–π^* transitions. Auxochromes are also present in most dyes that will influence the solubility of the dyes, for example, carboxylic acid group, amino group, sulfonic group, and hydroxyl group. Auxochromes cannot undergo π–π^* transitions but can undergo transition of n electrons.

4. Classification of dye(s)

Dye(s) are the organic compounds that will impart color to different substrates, which include paper, printing, textile, cosmetics, waxes, plastics, pharmaceuticals, and so on; there are two colorants present: dyes and pigments. Dyes are mostly soluble in water and diffuse into the material and are fixed for colorizing the material, whereas pigments are mostly insoluble in water and do not interact with the substrates. The preparation of the synthetic dyes involves the conversion of basic organic chemicals such as benzene, anthracene, and so on into dye intermediates through the addition of different functional groups such as nitro, amino, bromo, choloro, and so on [7]. Dyes are classified based on their chemical structure and color index (CI). Some common classes of dyes are mono-azo, di-azo, tri-azo, anthroquinone, triarylmethane, and phthalocyanines. Further, dyes can be classified based on the usage in textile industry such as anionic, cationic, and non-ionic (Fig. 1). On the basis of the color, dyes can be subclassified or subdivided into yellow, orange, red, violet, blue, green, and black [7].

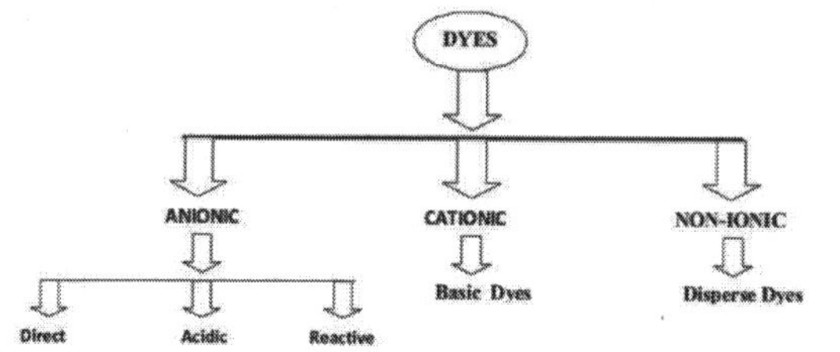

Figure 1. Classification of dye(s) [8].

Some properties of dyes classified on their usage [9–11] are discussed elaborately as follows:

1. Acid dyes: They are water-soluble anionic dyes in nature and negative in soluble form. The functional groups that are present in acidic dyes are azo (including premetallized), triphenylmethane, anthroquinone, azine, xanthene, nitro, and nitroso. They are made for dyeing of nylon, wool, and silk. However, it can be used for paper, leather, ink-jet printing, food, and cosmetics.

2. Cationic (basic) dyes: They are also soluble in water after modification. However, they produced colored cations in solution; therefore, it is also called cationic dyes. The functional groups that are present in basic dyes are triarylmethane, diazahemicyanine, cyanine, hemicyanine, thiazine, oxazine, and acridine. Basic dyes are extensively used for dyeing of jute, cut flowers, dried flower, coir, and so on.

3. Disperse dyes: They are almost insoluble in water and remained as suspended microscopic particles. These dyes are only effective for dyeing of polyester. Some types are also used for nylon and acetate. The functional groups remained for disperse dyes are azo, anthroquinone, styryl, nitro, and benzodifuranone.

4. Direct dyes: They are anionic dyes and normally applied together with electrolyte, sodium chloride, and sodium sulfate for high affinity to cellulosic fibers. These dyes are molecules that can hold on cellulosic fibers without help from other chemicals. They are used for dyeing of cotton, rayon, paper, leather, and nylon.

5. Reactive dyes: They create a covalent bond between the dye and the fiber. They exhibit a reactive group that may be haloheterocycle or an activated double bond. They are normally used in alkali condition through the formation of chemical bond with a hydroxyl group on the cellulosic fiber. It has been found that during application the chromophore group is activated and allowed to react to the surface of the substrate. It is used as colorant for dyeing of cotton and cellulosics.

6. Solvent dyes: They are normally soluble in organic solvents. They are used as colorants for organic solvents, hydrocarbon fuels, waxes, lubricants, and plastics. They are nonpolar and do not ionized in solution. The principal chemical groups are predominantly azo and anthroquinone, but phthalocyanines and triarylmethane dyes are also used.

7. Sulfur dyes: They are synthetic organic molecules used for the coloration of cellulosic fiber. These dyes contain sulfur group as chromophore. These are ionized through thionization or sulfurization of organic intermediates. They are not soluble in water and do not have any affinity for the cellulosic fiber. However, when treated with a weak alkaline solution of sodium sulfide or reducing agent to form a leuco compound that is soluble in water and has affinity to cellulosic materials. They are used for the coloration of cotton and rayon and have limited use with polyamide fibers, silk, leather, paper, and wood.

8. Vat dyes: They are normally insoluble in water. They are indigo and the anthraquinone derivatives, which are used for the coloration of cellulosic fibers. The dye is applied in a soluble or reduced form through the impregnation of fiber. It is further oxidized in the fiber back to its original insoluble form.

5. The production and discharge of dye(s)

More than 10,000 dyes are commercially available [12] and currently used in various materials such as textiles, paper, plastic, leather, food, drugs, and cosmetics [13]. In 2005, about 108 tonnes of dyestuffs were produced in the world. As textile industries have long been the largest consumer of dyes, it was foreseeable that the demand of dyes in the world will continue to rise in the forthcoming years because the fiber consumption has generally increased at a rate faster than the growth of population [6].

The rapid growth in the use of reactive dyes is due to the increasing use of cellulosic fibers and the technical and economic limitations of other dyes used for these fibers [14]. It is estimated that 2% of dyes produced annually are discharged in effluents from manufacturing operations, and 10% of dyes were discharged from textile and associated industries. Therefore, a large amount of dyes are lost into the effluents. The discharge of highly colored effluent is currently one of the major environmental problems. It can be seen that reactive dyes have rather low rates of fixation while the highest fixation rates are basic dyes. After the reactive dyeing process is complete, up to 800 mg/L of hydrolyzed dyes may remain in the bath. Therefore, a high concentration of reactive dyes is discharged into the effluent. In addition, reactive dyes are not easily biodegradable and thus may still remain in the effluent even after extensive treatment [15]. It has been found that large volumes of water and chemicals are normally required for textile industries. In consequence, huge unused dye(s) and auxiliary chemicals along with large amounts of water are found in wastewater streams from the textile dyeing operation. It has been reported that about 8–20% of the total pollution load was contributed due to incomplete exhaustion of the dyes. It is obviously true that the presence of dyes about as to 1 ppm in water is usually unacceptable [16].

6. The toxicity of dye(s)

Dye toxicity has been studied in many researches. The acute toxicity of dyes is generally low. Only a few dyes and pigments are considered to be carcinogenic by U.S. regulatory agencies. Among these are benzidine and benzidine congener dyes such as CI Direct Black 38, CI Acid Red 114, CI Direct Blue 15, and CI Direct Blue 218 [17]. Azo dyes contain one or more nitrogen–nitrogen double bonds (–N=N–) called azo groups in the chemical structure. Azo dyes are seldom directly mutagenic or carcinogenic except for some azo dyes with free amino groups [18]. Under reductive condition, the azo groups can be cleaved to form two aromatic amines.

After cleavage of azo linkages, toxic amines are released to water. These intermediate products cause severe detrimental effects on human beings and aquatic life. For human being, these intermediates damage the vital organs such as the brain, liver, kidneys, central nervous system, and reproductive system. However, they can also prevent photosynthetic activity by reducing light penetration. In this way, the hazardous effects of dye(s) peculate from their discharge point to receive water. Therefore, it is urged for researchers to find out the way for removal of such toxic components in industrialized countries in the world [19]. Wastewater treatment is a difficult task by conventional methods such as physical, chemical, and biological due to its complex molecular structure of dyes. Some new technologies are being investigated by which decoloration of the problem could be solved.

7. Pollution from the dye-containing effluents

The colored effluent brings a negative esthetic effect on the wastewater because the color can also be observed by our eyes even when the concentration is less than 1 ppm. In addition, the absorption and reflection of sunlight by the colored effluents affect the water transparency and gas solubility of water bodies. The heavy-metal ions from textile effluents have also been reported at high concentrations in both algae and higher plants [20]. Even worse, some of the dyes and their biodegraded products are also toxic, carcinogenic, and mutagenic [17].

Sometimes, it has been found that due to the accessibility of small-scale industries in the greater extent, it was stared the decentralized treatment methods for individual industry. As the treatment process for such toxic pollutants in proper manner is an expensive, they are eventually discarded into the environment that is about 40% of the total industrial wastewater. As far the environmental protection is an urgent issue in connection with industrial development, it promotes to develop eco-friendly technologies that will reduce the consumption of freshwater and lower output of wastewater. The release of important amounts of synthetic dyes to the environment causes public concern and minimizes legislation problems [21,22].

8. Dye removal techniques

The strategy for removal of dyes and pigments from textile effluents is just a simple separation process from a purely engineering point of view. Theoretically, there is a great number of separation processes tailored to the removal of a specific compound. Dye-containing wastewater can be treated in different ways such as physical, chemical, and biological approaches. Physical treatment methods employ the application of physical forces for the separation of dyes from wastewater. Physical methods include different precipitation methods (such as coagulation, flocculation, and sedimentation), adsorption (on a wide variety of inorganic and organic supports), filtration, reverse osmosis, ultra filtration, and nanofiltration. However, chemical method is brought about by the addition of chemicals or by chemical reactions (such as reduction, oxidation, complex metric methods, ion exchange, and neutralization). However, biological treatments normally carried out aerobically or anaerobically that will depend on the presence or absence of oxygen to the system. Biological treatments happen in the presence of biological catalyst that stimulates the degradation are also called biodegradation. Chemical treatment methods are normally carried out by the addition of chemicals through chemical reaction such as reduction, oxidation, complex metric methods, ion exchange, and neutralization [23]. It may eventually generate toxic intermediate products. It is obviously true that the treatment of colored wastewaters depends not only on ecological parameters such as chemical oxygen demand (COD), biological oxygen demand, total organic carbon, absorbable organic halide, temperature, and pH but also on initial dye concentrations in wastewaters [23]. The entire process is considered environmentally friendly when the by-product stream has negligible environmental effects. Otherwise, additional treatment is required, and the problem of the removal of the hazardous compounds from the raw influent has been just relocated.

8.1. Physical treatment

8.1.1. Coagulation–flocculation

Coagulation–flocculation methods were successfully applied for color removal of sulfur and disperse dyes, whereas acid, direct, reactive, and vat dyes presented very low coagulation–

flocculation capacity. Coagulant agents that are normally used for decolorization of colorants are aluminum sulfate, ferrous, ferric sulfate, ferric chloride, calcium chloride, and copper sulfate as well as several co-polymers such as penta ethylene, hexamine, and ethylediene dichloride. The mechanism behind this coagulation process is by the formation of flocs with the dyes, which can be separated by filtration or sedimentation [23]. Polyelectrolyte can also be dosed during the flocculation phase to improve the floc settleability [24]. It is obviously advantageous that there is no question of decomposition of dyes, which can produce more potentially harmful and toxic compound. In addition, only separation of colorants has been taken place, which is economic. However, the production of sludge is only disadvantage for coagulation–flocculation processes [25].

In coagulation process, chemicals are rapidly dispersed in wastewaters, which can change the characteristics of the suspended particles such that they tend to coalesce and form flocs that sink rapidly. Conventional physical process is not efficiently separate the negatively charged colloidal suspensions. However, the decoloration of effluent stream can be made economically through the application of coagulation process. Coagulation process is normally carried out by the addition of positive ions that will reduce the electro kinetic repulsion between the particles. It has been reported by Marmagne and Coste that the color removal of sulfur dyes can be efficiently carried out by coagulation. They did their experiment in bench flocculators. The good-quality flocs were produced; therefore, minimum time was taken for settling. It was reported that the removal efficiency in terms of COD and color was found to be 83.9% and 96.1%, respectively [26,27]. Coagulation process is also affected by the chemicals, pH, and temperature of the system [27].

8.1.2. Filtration technology

The filtration technology is the prime module that is used in drinking water and wastewater treatment. This technology constitutes microfiltration, ultrafiltration, nanofiltration, and reverses osmosis. For the removal of the color, this technology showed some promising results. Individual membrane is significant for the water treatment process. Microfiltration is not suited for the wastewater treatment due to its large pore size; nanofiltration and ultrafiltration are efficiently remove different sorts of dyes. Generally, the dye molecule clogged in the membrane and limits the separation process for the usage of dyeing effluent treatments. The limitation of this process is its high pressure, momentous energy consumption, cost of membrane is high, and life span is also short, and these properties are creating hindrance for the treatment of dyestuff or organic pollutant removal. The reverse osmosis process is better for rejecting salts. It gives better results in decolorizing and desalting against various dye effluents and can be applied for recycling. The treated wastewater is near to pure water.

8.1.3. Adsorption

Adsorption is the process in which dissolved molecules are attached to the surface of an adsorbent by physical and chemical forces. Adsorption by activated carbon has been widely used for wastewater treatment. Activated carbon and other materials can remove the dyes in the wastewater, either by adsorption or by combined adsorption and ion exchange. Adsorption gives good results and has gained favor recently due to its ability to remove different types of dyes, excellent adsorption ability [28,29], ease of operation, and insensitivity to toxic pollutants and can be used in fixed bed columns for treating the water continuously [30]. However, its widespread use is restricted due to high cost [31]. Therefore, researchers have been looking for low cost adsorbents as alternatives to activated carbon.

8.2. Chemical treatment

Chemical treatment of the wastewater is carried out with the help of coagulants and flocculants, and it gives quiet promising results. Chemicals that are being used in this treatment are aluminum, calcium, and ferric ions for the removal of the dye effluents and induce flocculation. For the betterment of the process, the combination of two might be used to augment the process. Sometimes, the process is economically sound, but, in some instances, it could be expensive due to the price of the chemicals. The process gives satisfactory removal of disperse, vat, and sulfur dyes. However, the limitation of this technique is the production of concentrated sludge in large quantity, and the removal of reactive, azo, and basic dyes by this technique is not at par or up to the mark.

8.2.1. Oxidation

Oxidation is the one of the most commonly used chemical decoloration process due to its simplicity of application. Oxidation processes can include oxidation through biological organisms, ozone, sodium hypochlorite, hydrogen peroxide, and even acids. The oxidative process will produce smaller molecules because the dyes are broken down. Conventional oxidation treatments are incapable to oxidize dyes (mainly for removing color) and toxic organic compounds completely from textile effluents. The above-mentioned limitation can overcome through the development of advanced oxidation processes (AOPs) where the generation of free hydroxyl radicals (OH) takes place. It is obviously true that these free radicals increase the rate of reaction with several folds when compared with normal oxidants. OHs can oxidize both the dyes and the toxic organic compounds that normally cannot be oxidized by conventional oxidants [25]. In AOPs, oxidizing agents such as ozone and hydrogen peroxide are used with catalysts (such as Fe, Mn, and TiO_2) either in the presence or in the absence of an irradiation source [24]. Chemical oxidation removes the dyes from the dye-containing effluent by oxidation, resulting in aromatic ring cleavage of the dye molecules [32].

8.3. Biological techniques

Recent application of several physicochemical methods has been used for azo dye decolorization, but these methods are expensive and produce large amounts of sludge after treatment. Extensively used coagulation or flocculation techniques create or generate large amounts of sludge that requires safe disposal. Adsorption and, to a certain extent, membrane filtration techniques lead to secondary waste streams that need further treatment. There are many reports on the use of physicochemical methods for color removal from dye-containing effluents [33–35] apart from that present scenario biological treatment methods are most suitable and widely used due to their cost effectiveness, ability to produce less sludge, and eco-friendly nature [36,37].

Bioremediation is normally carried out by the use of microorganisms to remove the pollution from the environment, which is a key research area in the environmental engineering [38]. In such approaches, microorganisms adapt themselves to the toxic wastes and develop into new resistant strains naturally, which then transform various toxic chemicals into less harmful forms. The mechanism behind the biodegradation of recalcitrant compounds in the microbial system is based on the action of the biotransformation enzymes [39]. Several reports demonstrate the degradation of complex organic substances that can be brought about by enzymatic mechanisms, such as those associated with laccase [40], lignin peroxidas [41], NADH–DCIP reductase [42], tyrosinase [43], hexane oxidase [39], and aminopyrine *N*-demethylase [44]. There are several treatment approaches successfully applied by the biotechnologists to remove the dyes from effluent streams with regard to tackling azo dye pollution in an eco-efficient manner. It is reported that the use of bacteria followed by physicochemical processes may used for successful removal of azo dyes. As azo dyes are xenobiotic in nature and recalcitrant to biodegradation, the use of microbial or enzymatic treatment method may be useful for the complete removal or degradation of such dyes from textile effluent. In this approach, several advantages have eco-friendly, inexpensive, and less sludge production. In addition, the intermediate products that are formed are nontoxic due to complete mineralization, and the process requires less water consumption when compared with physicochemical methods [38]. The effectiveness of microbial decolorization depends on the adaptability and the activity of the selected microorganisms. Consequently, a large number of species have been tested for the decolorization and mineralization of various dyes in recent years [45]. The isolation of potent species and their degradation is one of the interesting biological aspects of effluent treatment [46]. A wide variety of microorganisms are capable of decolorizing a wide range of dyes, including bacteria [39], fungi [47], yeasts [48], actinomycetes [48,49], and algae [50].

8.3.1. Decolorization and degradation of dyes by plants (phytoremediation)

Phytoremediation is an emerging technology that promises the effective and inexpensive approach for the remediation of soils and groundwater contaminated with heavy metals and organic pollutants [51]. As phytoremediation is an autotrophic system and requires little nutrient input, the main advantages of phytoremediation are easier to manage and accepted by public due to both of its esthetic appeal and environmental sustainability [38,52]. More specifically, narrow-leaved cattails have been studied in synthetic reactive dye wastewater treatment under caustic conditions [53,54], where approximately 72–77% can be reduced with coco yam plants. It has been reported that the three plant species namely *Brassica juncea*, *Sorghum vulgare*, and *Phaseolusmungo* from different agronomic consequences have been used to evaluate the decolorization efficiency by using azo dyes in textile effluent. It has been reported that *B. juncea*, *S. vulgare*, and *P. mungo* showed 79%, 57%, and 53% efficiency, respectively [38,55]. Similarly, an herb *Blumea malcommi* was found to degrade textile dyes (Reactive Red 5B). Extensive research has been undertaken to develop effective and efficient phytoremediation techniques. It was reported that hairy root cultures of *Tagetes patula* L.

(Marigold) are effective in the decolorization of Reactive Red 198, and the enzyme system in the plant responsible for this was determined [51]. However, there are several disadvantages related to large-scale phytoremediation process. It includes pollutants tolerance by the plant, the bioavailable fraction of the contaminants along with the transpiration of volatile organic pollutants and large areas to implant the treatment [38,56].

8.3.2. Microbial treatment

Microorganisms are already present in the wastewater treatment feed on the complex substances in the wastewater, converting them into simpler substances, improvement treatment. The biological treatment is nowadays common and extensive technique employed in dye wastewater treatment. There are several reports where a huge number of species have been used for the removal and complete mineralization of different sorts of dyes. The main advantage of this process is inexpensive, low running costs, and nontoxic end products. However, these process may be aerobic (in the presence of oxygen), anaerobic (without oxygen), or combined aerobic–anaerobic. Bacteria and fungi are normally used in aerobic treatment for their ability to treat dye wastewaters [11].

8.3.2.1. Aerobic treatment

In aerobic treatment, enzymes secreted by bacteria present in the wastewater breakdown the organic compounds. The work to identify and isolate aerobic bacteria capable of degrading various dyes has been going on since more than two decades. A number of triphenylmethane dyes, such as magenta, crystal violet, pararosaniline, brilliant green, malachite green, and ethyl violet, have been found to be efficiently decolorized (92–100%) by the strain *Kurthia* sp. It was reported by the researchers that after biotransformation, the extent of COD reduction of the cell free extracts of triphenylmethane dyes was more than 88% in all dyes except in the case of ethyl violet (70%). Since last two decades, various researchers have investigated *Phanerochaete chrysosporium*, among various fungi, extensively for its ability to decolorize a wide range of dyes. Besides this, microorganisms including *Rhyzopus oryzae, Cyathus bulleri, Coriolus versicolour, Funalia trogii, Laetiporous sulphureus, Streptomyces* sp., *Trametes versicolour*, and so on have also been tested for the decolorization of dyes. It has been found that different operating parameters such as initial concentration of pollutants, initial pH, and temperature of the effluent affect the removal process. Several strategies may be used after fungal treatment. It has been reported thatthe treatability of the effluent by other microorganisms can be improvedfor satisfactory removal of dyes. It is obviously true that these techniques are suitable for some dyes; however, most of the dyes are recalcitrant to biological breakdown or are nontransformable under aerobic conditions [11].

8.3.2.2. Anaerobic treatment

The anaerobic treatment is quiet promising for the degradation of an extensive range of synthetic dyes has been well demonstrated and established. From the literature, it has been reported that under anaerobic conditions, some dyes have been degraded or mineralized. Since last few decades, researchers reported that decolorization of azo dyes showed some positive result in case of mordant orange-1 and azo-disalicylate could be reduced and decolorized under anaerobic conditions using methanogenic granular sludge. Another study proved the feasibility of the application of anaerobic granular sludge for the total decolorization of 20 azo dyes. An anaerobic pre-treatment step could be a cheap alternative compared with aerobic systems as expensive aeration is absent and problems with bulking sludge are avoided. It is reported that anaerobic treatment of effluent for dye removal can be efficiently carried out; however, heavy metals can be retained through sulfate reduction. In addition, due to foaming problems, associat for surfactants and high effluent temperatures along with high pH is the main limitation for degradation of dyes. Nevertheless, it is also mentioned that BOD removal can be insufficient; dyes and other refractory organics are not mineralized; nutrients (N and P) are not removed; and sulfates give rise to sulfides [11].

8.3.2.3. Combined aerobic–anaerobic treatment

For the better removal of dyestuff from the wastewater of textile effluent, the combination of aerobic and anaerobic treatments may give promising results. It is advantageous because the complete mineralization is achieved due to the synergistic action of different organisms. It has been reported that the reduction of the azo bond can be achieved under the reducing conditions in anaerobic bioreactors. In consequence, colorless aromatic amines may be formed, which are mineralized under aerobic conditions. Therefore, the combined anaerobic–aerobic azo dye treatment system is an attractive approach for the researchers [11]. Thus, an anaerobic decolorization followed by aerobic post-treatment is generally recommended for treating dye wastewaters. Generally, the operating conditions such as initial concentration of dyes, initial pH of solution, and temperature of the effluent play an important role for decolorization of dyes. In addition, this technique is cost competitive and suitable for various dyes. However, the main limitation of the biological treatment is low biodegradability, less flexibility in design and operation, larger land area requirement, and longer times required for decolorization processes. Therefore, it is an urge for scientist for removal of dyes from effluent on a continuous basis in liquid-state fermentations [11].

8.3.2.4. Enzyme-mediated dye removal

From the literature, it has been found that the white-rot fungi, which produce nonspecific extracellular ligninolytic enzymes are most efficient to remove synthetic dyes. These enzymes are lignin peroxidase (ligninase, LiP, EC 1.11.1.14), manganese peroxidase (MnP, EC 1.11.1.13), and copper-containing laccase (benzenediol:oxygen oxidoreductase, EC 1.10.3.2). Of these enzymes, laccases (EC 1.10.3.2) have great potential in bioremediation due to their ability to oxidize a broad range of substrates. Laccases belong to the group of oxidases, which contain four copper atoms in their catalytic site. The capability of laccases to degrade phenolic compounds makes them suitable for the degradation of xenobiotic compounds in the treatment of wastewaters [57].

There is an extensive research carried out for laccase-mediated dye removal using wild strain owing to their potential industrial applications. Screening of proper microorganism is important criteria to get the desired product. The microorganism that will be used for laccase production should produce adequate yields and should not produce toxins or any other undesired products. The main challenges using wild strain are the availability of potent microbial strain and the application of this biocatalyst for industrial-scale dye removal [58]. It is also important to note that this strain should be robust under industrial conditions. It is advantageous that there is no batch-to-batch variation of laccase production found using wild strain. However, low yield is main drawback for laccase production using wild strain. In addition, the isolation of potent strain for removal of dyes is tedious and time consuming. The microbial diversity during the degradation of dyes under natural conditions needs to be evaluated, and the isolation, screening, and characterization of new well-adapted microbial strains are used to potentially improve enzyme production.

The main challenges for the engineered strategy include the availability of tools that can be modified by recombinant DNA technology and the application of these tools, so that a desired laccase will be produced with high yield and robustness under industrial conditions. In this strategy, the enzyme that is more suitable for industrial applications has been chosen [59]. The main challenge for recombinant DNA technology is to improve the fermentation characteristics of genetically engineered organisms by introducing genes. It has been found that the robustness of engineered laccase enzymes is often required for industrial applications. There are several reports where cloning of laccase gene, random mutagenesis, site-specific mutagenesis, or the combination of both have been frequently used to get robust engineered laccase enzymes for industrial applications [60]. Iterative saturation mutagenesis (ISM) is a directed evolution method to improve the favorable characteristics of enzymes. The repetitive cycles of saturation mutagenesis are applied in ISM at chosen sites of two or three amino acids of the protein and protein structure. Beneficial mutations were found by performing 3–4 rounds of ISM, and these beneficial mutations are systematically incorporated into the libraries [61]. The grafting of the above three enzymes [lignin peroxidase (ligninase, LiP, EC 1.11.1.14), manganese peroxidase (MnP, EC 1.11.1.13), and copper-containing laccase (benzenediol:oxygen oxidoreductase, EC 1.10.3.2)] to chimeric enzymes could be the alternative path to improve the efficiency of the bioprocess and cost-effective dye removal. In addition, it also decreases the required cost of the applied enzymes. It is obvious that the primary goal is to decrease the process cost of the overall bioprocess. In the 21st century, the development of bioprocesses has been focused on enzyme mediated bioprocess, which is an attractive tool to reach the economical and ecological goals.

There are several papers published on cellular recognition of dyes through genetic regulation and expression of laccase enzyme in presence of such complex organic compounds. It has been found that laccases are synthesized when microorganisms are cultured on dyes because it induced the activity of enzyme complexes in microorganisms [62]. It is interested to note that dyes did not directly enter inside the cell to influence the regulation of gene and the expression of laccase enzyme. As enzyme secretion is an induction process, there should be a physical contact between part of the regulatory machinery of the cell and the inducer. The inducers have some recognition site on the surface of cell that regulates the process. The expressed enzyme will secrete extracellularlly and hydrolyze the complex structure that can be easily transported inside.

A fermentation process involving microbial cells requires the investigation of raw materials, biomass, and how they are treated and mixed with other ingredients required for cells to grow well. A pure strain of a microorganism is normally introduced into the vessel. The bioreactor supports the natural process by providing suitable conditions such as optimum temperature, pH, nutritional elements, enabling cells to grow and form metabolites and enzymes. The cells will start to multiply exponentially after a certain period of lag time and reach a maximum cell concentration as the medium is depleted. In addition, the fermentation process may be constituted anywhere between 5% and 50% of the total fixed and operating costs of the process that is basically different depending on the type of product, the concentration level it produces, and the purity desired [63]. Therefore, optimal design and operation of a bioreactor frequently dominate the overall technological and economic performance of the process. To carry out a bioprocess on a large scale, it is necessary to investigate and develop three principle areas. To obtain a potent biocatalyst (such as microorganisms, animal cell, plant cell, or enzyme) along with medium, optimization is a primary criterion for a fermentation process. In addition, it is required to create the best possible environment for the catalyst to perform by designing the bioreactor and operating it in the most efficient way. However, low stability and high production cost are the key factors for the application of free enzyme for dye removal. However, the immobilized laccase-based system can overcome the limitations such as low stability and high production cost. The stability of enzyme in extreme environment condition or in the presence of chemical is the main advantage of immobilized system. It is also obvious that immobilized laccase can be separated easily from the reaction, allowing the enzymes can be used in continuous manner [64,65].

Recently, Kaushik et al. (2014) experimented with *Aspergillus lentulus* for the production of xylanase through solid state fermentation. In this experiment, various low-cost agro residues were used as substrate. The maximum xylanase production (158.4 U/g) was reported on the 4th day of incubation where wheat bran was used as the substrate. However, 153.0 U/g, 129.9 U/g, and 49.4 U/g of xylanase production were achieved in presence corn cob, sugarcane bagasse, and wheat straw as substrate, respectively. It was experimented to solve the problem associated with pulp and paper industries to control pollution that is due to pulp bleaching and release of colored wastewater [65]. The enzyme showed good stability at high pH and temperature (>75% activity retained at pH 9 and 70°C). They also experimented to remove anionic (>85.0% removal) and cationic (>96.0% removal) dyes. It was revealed that dye removal can be possible significantly to meet the requirements of pulp and bleaching industries through an effective and sustainable approach [66].

9. Conclusion

There are, however, various technological and economic obstacles that have to be overcome before industrial-scale enzyme-mediated dye removal can take place. The selection and successful large-scale cultivation of strain for maximum enzyme production remain a major upstream challenge. On the other hand, the development of an effective genetic-engineered strain is critical for the successful fermentation processes. Despite the routine use of laboratory-scale cloning, the variables affecting recombinant strain are not well understood, and no method for industrial scale is currently established. This manuscript attempts to address the knowledge gap surrounding enzyme-mediated bioprocess technology for development of commercial dye removal process from textile effluent.

References

[1] D.W. O'Connell, C. Birkinshaw, T.F. O'Dwyer. Heavy metal adsorbents prepared from the modification of cellulose: a review. Bioresource Technology 2008; 99: 6709–6724.

[2] A. Gomes, R. Brás, M. Ferra, M. Amorim, R. Porter. Biological treatment of effluent containing textile dyes. Coloration Technology 2000; 116: 393–397.

[3] C. O'Neill, F.R. Hawkes, D.L. Hawkes, N.D. Lourenco, H.M. Pinheiro, W. Delee. Colour in textile effluents–sources, measurement, discharge consents and simulation: a review. Journal of Chemical Technology and Biotechnology 1999; 74: 1009–1018.

[4] I.M. Banat, P. Nigam, D. Singh, R. Marchant. Microbial decolorization of textile-dye-containing effluents: a review. Bioresource Technology 1996; 58: 217–227.

[5] Č. Novotný, N. Dias, A. Kapanen, K. Malachová, M. Vándrovcová, M. Itävaara, N. Lima. Comparative use of bacterial, algal and protozoan tests to study toxicity of azo-and anthraquinone dyes. Chemosphere 2006; 63: 1436–1442.

[6] R.E. Kirk, D.F. Othmer, K. Othmer, Encyclopedia of Chemical Technology, Wiley, New York, 2006.

[7] R. Ramanath. Color: An Introduction to Practice and Principles. Wiley Online Library, USA, 2005.

[8] Y. Fu, T. Viraraghavan. Fungal decolorization of dye wastewaters: a review. Bioresource Technology 2001; 79: 251–262.

[9] K. Hunger. Industrial Dyes: Chemistry, Properties, Application. Wiley Online Library, USA, 2003.

[10] R. Christie. Why is indigo blue? Biotechnic & Histochemistry 2007; 82: 51–56.

[11] V. Gupta. Application of low-cost adsorbents for dye removal – a review. Journal of Environmental Management 2009; 90: 2313–2342.

[12] H. Zollinger. Color Chemistry: Syntheses, Properties, and Applications of Organic Dyes and Pigments, Wiley, Zurich, 2003.

[13] E. Forgacs, T. Cserhati, G. Oros. Removal of synthetic dyes from wastewaters: a review. Environment International 2004; 30: 953–971.

[14] S.J. Allen, B. Kowmanova. Decolorization of water/wastewater using adsorption. Journal of the University of Chemical Technology and Metallurgy 2005; 40: 175–192.

[15] P. Cooper. Removing colour from dyehouse wastewaters – a critical review of technology available. Journal of the Society of Dyers and Colourists 1993; 109: 97–100.

[16] B. Noroozi, G. Sorial, H. Bahrami, M. Arami. Adsorption of binary mixtures of cationic dyes. Dyes and Pigments 2008; 76: 784–791.

[17] A. Freeman, H.S. Reife. Environmental Chemistry of Dyes and Pigments, Wiley, New York, 1996.

[18] H. Kusic, D. Juretic, N. Koprivanac, V. Marin, A.L. Bozic. Photooxidation processes for an azo dye in aqueous media: modeling of degradation kinetic and ecological parameters evaluation. Journal of Hazardous Materials 2011; 185: 1558–1568.

[19] C.F. Iscen, I. Kiran, S. Ilhan. Biosorption of Reactive Black 5 dye by *Penicillium restrictum*: the kinetic study. Journal of Hazardous Materials 2007; 143: 335–340.

[20] I.M. Banat, P. Nigam, D. Singh, R. Marchant. Marchant, microbial decolorization of textile-dye-containing effluents: a review. Bioresource Technology 1996; 58: 217–227.

[21] P. Kaushik, A. Malik. Fungal dye decolourization: recent advances and future potential. Environment International 2009; 35: 127–141.

[22] Available at: www.intechopen.com.

[23] Available at: www.eprints.utar.edu.my.

[24] E. Forgacs, T. Cserhati, G. Oros. Removal of synthetic dyes from wastewaters: a review. Environment International 2004; 30: 953–971.

[25] J.V. Valh, A.M. Le Marechal, S. Vajnhandl, T. Jerič, E. Šimon. Water in the textile industry. Treatise on Water Science 2011; 4: 685–706.

[26] O. Marmagne, C. Coste. Color removal from textile plant effluents. American Dyestuff Reporter 1996; 85: 6.

[27] T.A. Nguyen, R.-S. Juang. Treatment of waters and wastewaters containing sulfur dyes: a review. Chemical Engineering Journal 2013; 219: 109–117.

[28] K.K.H. Choy, G. McKay, J.F. Porter. Sorption of acid dyes from effluents using activated carbon. Resources Conservation and Recycling 1999; 27: 57–71.

[29] Y.S. Ho, G. McKay. Sorption of dyes and copper ions onto biosorbents. Process Biochemistry 2003; 38: 1047–1061.

[30] K. Chwalisz, S. Shao-Qing, R.E. Garfield, H.M. Beier. Cervical ripening in guinea-pigs after a local application of nitric oxide. Human Reproduction 1997; 12: 2093–2101.

[31] G. Crini. Non-conventional low-cost adsorbents for dye removal: a review. Bioresource Technology 2006; 97: 1061–1085.

[32] C. Raghavacharya. Colour removal from industrial effluents: a comparative review of available technologies. Chemical Engineering World 1997; 32: 53–54.

[33] V. López-Grimau, M. Gutierrez. Decolourisation of simulated reactive dyebath effluents by electrochemical oxidation assisted by UV light. Chemosphere 2006; 62: 106–112.

[34] V. Golob, A. Vinder, M. Simonič. Efficiency of the coagulation/flocculation method for the treatment of dyebath effluents. Dyes and Pigments 2005; 67: 93–97.

[35] K. Swaminathan, S. Sandhya, A.C. Sophia, K. Pachhade, Y. Subrahmanyam. Decolorization and degradation of H-acid and other dyes using ferrous–hydrogen peroxide system. Chemosphere 2003; 50: 619–625.

[36] H. Chen. Recent advances in azo dye degrading enzyme research. Current Protein and Peptide Science 2006; 7: 101–111.

[37] Z.-Y. Song, J.-T. Zhou, J. Wang, B. Yan, C.-H. Du. Decolorization of azo dyes by *Rhodobacter sphaeroides*. Biotechnology Letters 2003; 25: 1815–1818.

[38] R. Saratale, G. Saratale, J. Chang, S. Govindwar. Bacterial decolorization and degradation of azo dyes: a review. Journal of the Taiwan Institute of Chemical Engineers 2011; 42: 138–157.

[39] G. Saratale, S. Kalme, S. Bhosale, S. Govindwar. Biodegradation of kerosene by *Aspergillus ochraceus* NCIM-1146. Journal of Basic Microbiology 2007; 47: 400–405.

[40] N. Hatvani, I. Mécs. Production of laccase and manganese peroxidase by *Lentinus edodes* on malt-containing by-product of the brewing process. Process Biochemistry 2001; 37: 491–496.

[41] N. Duran, E. Esposito. Potential applications of oxidative enzymes and phenoloxidase-like compounds in wastewater and soil treatment: a review. Applied Catalysis B: Environmental 2000; 28: 83–99.

[42] S. Bhosale, G. Saratale, S. Govindwar. Biotransformation enzymes in *Cunninghamella blakesleeana* (NCIM-687). Journal of Basic Microbiology 2006; 46: 444–448.

[43] X. Zhang, W.H. Flurkey. Phenoloxidases in Portabella mushrooms. Journal of Food Science 1997; 62: 97–100.

[44] M. Salokhe, S. Govindwar. Effect of carbon source on the biotransformation enzymesin *Serratia marcescens*. World Journal of Microbiology and Biotechnology 1999; 15: 259–263.

[45] A. Pandey, P. Singh, L. Iyengar. Bacterial decolorization and degradation of azo dyes. International Biodeterioration & Biodegradation 2007; 59: 73–84.

[46] B.-Y. Chen, W.-M. Chen, F.-L. Wu, P.-K. Chen, C.-Y. Yen. Revealing azo-dye decolorization of indigenous *Aeromonas hydrophila* from fountain spring in Northeast Taiwan. Journal of the Chinese Institute of Chemical Engineers 2008; 39: 495–501.

[47] R. Humnabadkar, G. Saratale, S. Govindwar. Decolorization of purple 2R by *Aspergillus ochraceus* (NCIM-1146). Asian Journal of Microbiology Biotechnology & Environmental Science 2008; 10: 693–697.

[48] R. Saratale, G. Saratale, J.-S. Chang, S. Govindwar. Decolorization and biodegradation of textile dye Navy blue HER by *Trichosporon beigelii* NCIM-3326. Journal of Hazardous Materials 2009; 166: 1421–1428.

[49] K.M. Machado, L.C. Compart, R.O. Morais, L.H. Rosa, M.H. Santos. Biodegradation of reactive textile dyes by basidiomycetous fungi from Brazilian ecosystems. Brazilian Journal of Microbiology 2006; 37: 481–487.

[50] V. Gupta, A. Rastogi, V. Saini, N. Jain. Biosorption of copper (II) from aqueous solutions by *Spirogyra* species. Journal of Colloid and Interface Science 2006; 296: 59–63.

[51] P. Patil, N. Desai, S. Govindwar, J.P. Jadhav, V. Bapat. Degradation analysis of Reactive Red 198 by hairy roots of *Tagetes patula* L. (Marigold). Planta 2009; 230: 725–735.

[52] A.N. Kagalkar, U.B. Jagtap, J.P. Jadhav, V.A. Bapat, S.P. Govindwar. Biotechnological strategies for phytoremediation of the sulfonated azo dye Direct Red 5B using *Blumea malcolmii* Hook. Bioresource Technology 2009; 100: 4104–4110.

[53] S. Nilratnisakorn, P. Thiravetyan, W. Nakbanpote. Synthetic reactive dye wastewater treatment by narrow-leaved cattails (*Typha angustifolia* Linn.): effects of dye, salinity and metals. Science Total Environment 2007; 384: 67–76.

[54] S.E. Mbuligwe. Comparative treatment of dye-rich wastewater in engineered wetland systems (EWSs) vegetated with different plants. Water Resources 2005; 39: 271–280.

[55] G.S. Ghodake, A.A. Talke, J.P. Jadhav, S.P. Govindwar. Potential of *Brassica juncea* in order to treat textile—effluent—contaminated sites. International Journal of Phytoremediation 2009; 11: 297–312.

[56] G. Ghodake, S. Jadhav, V. Dawkar, S. Govindwar. Biodegradation of diazo dye Direct brown MR by *Acinetobacter calcoaceticus* NCIM 2890. International Biodeterioration & Biodegradation 2009; 63: 433–439.

[57] S. Chakraborty, B. Basak, S. Dutta, B. Bhunia, A. Dey. Decolorization and biodegradation of congo red dye by a novel white rot fungus *Alternaria alternata* CMERI F6. Bioresource Technology 2013; 147: 662–666.

[58] U.S. Uday, P. Choudhury, T.K. Bandyopadhyay, B. Bhunia. Classification, mode of action and production strategy of xylanase and its application for biofuel production from water hyacinth. International Journal of Biological Macromolecules 2016; 82: 1041–1054.

[59] Q.K. Beg, M. Kapoor, L. Mahajan, G.S. Hoondal. Microbial xylanases and their industrial applications: a review. Applied Microbiology and Biotechnology 2001; 56: 326–338.

[60] P.A. Dalby. Engineering enzymes for biocatalysis. Recent Patents on Biotechnology 2007; 1: 1–9.

[61] M.T. Reetz, J.D. Carballeira. Iterative saturation mutagenesis (ISM) for rapid directed evolution of functional enzymes. Nature Protocols 2007; 2: 891–903.

[62] P. Biely. Biochemical aspects of the production of microbial hemicellulases. Hemicellulose and Hemicellulases. In: Hemicellulose and hemicellulases. eds Coughlan M. P.,Hazlewood&G. P. Portland Press, London, England, 1993, pp 29–51.

[63] Availbale at: www.fbae.org.

[64] C. Fersi, L. Gzara, M. Dhahbi. Treatment of textile effluents by membrane technologies. Desalination 2005; 185: 399–409.

[65] M. Fernández-Fernández, M.Á. Sanromán, D. Moldes. Recent developments and applications of immobilized laccase. Biotechnology Advances 2013; 31: 1808–1825.

[66] P. Kaushik, A. Mishra, A. Malik. Dual application of agricultural residues for xylanase production and dye removal through solid state fermentation. International Biodeterioration & Biodegradation 2014; 96: 1–8.

Chapter 5

Heterogeneous Photocatalysis Remediation of Wastewater Polluted by Indigoid Dyes

Abstract

Organic dyes constitute one of the largest groups of wastewater's pollutants. In general, they are released into the environment by textile industries. Approximately 100,000 dyes are widely used in the textile industry, and a large wastewater of dyestuff is generated annually. Among these, indigoid class is commercial dyes used mostly for cotton cloth dyeing. Indigo carmine (IC) is also one of the oldest dyes and still one of the most used in textile industry and is considered as a very toxic indigoid dye. Most toxic dyes are recalcitrant to biodegradation, causing a decrease in the efficiency of biological wastewater treatment plants. Titanium dioxide is a well-known photocatalyst mostly used in suspensions in photoreactions for wastewater treatment. The use of TiO_2 has some advantages such as ease of handling, low cost, low toxicity, high photochemical reactivity, and non-specific oxidative attack ability. In this way, it can promote the degradation of different target organic compounds with little change of operational parameters. The aim of this chapter is to present the different approaches already used in our team for the remediation of waters containing IC mainly through heterogeneous photocatalysis with TiO_2. Adsorption over activated carbon (AC) and photocatalytic degradation of IC mediated by titanium dioxide will be revised as well as some studies on the phototoxicity of the photoproducts with aquatic and terrestrial organisms. This chapter makes a comprehensive approach to the different results on the remediation of model effluents containing IC undertaken by this team of researchers.

Keywords: photocatalysis, titanium dioxide, wastewater treatment, Indigo carmine, ecotoxicology

1. Introduction

Textile industry process generates a significant amount of wastewaters containing 5–15% of an untreated dye, which can be released into the environment. Around 100,000 dyes are currently in use by the global textile industry, and 7×10^5 ton of dyestuff is produced annually worldwide. Moreover, the effluent of textile industries has intense color, chemical oxygen demand (COD), suspended solids, and several refractory compounds like heavy metals [1]. Discharges of untreated dye effluent into the water body produce colored effluents that not only cause esthetic deterioration but also affect oxygen and nitrogen cycles through photosynthesis, and they may also be toxic to aquatic biota [2]. Indigo is a commercial dye used mostly for cotton cloth dyeing (blue jeans), and the main constituent is indigotin that is extracted from the leaves of *Indigofera tinctoria* [3–5]. Indigo carmine (IC; 3,3-dioxo-2,2-bis-indolyden-5,5-disulfonic acid disodium salt) is also one of the oldest dyes and still employed extensively today for dyeing cotton with annual consumption around 33 million kg [6]. The wastewater-containing indigo is characterized by a dark blue color due to cross-conjugated system or H-chromophore, consisting of a single –C=C– double bond substituted by two NH donor groups and two CO acceptor groups [7]. The structure of IC is shown in Figure 1.

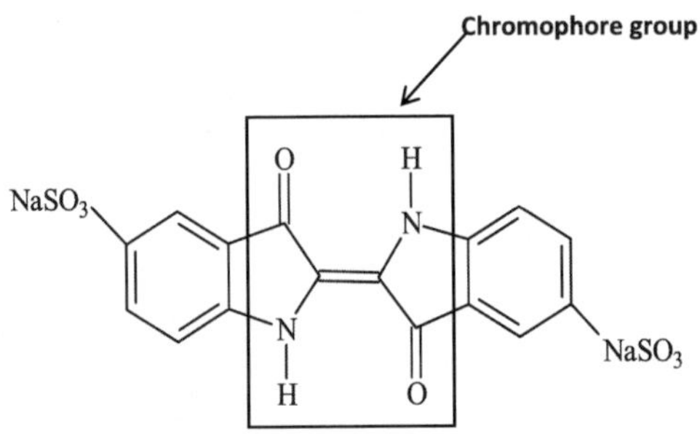

Figure 1. Chemical structure of Indigo carmine.

IC is a toxic dye once its contact with skin and eyes can cause permanent injury to cornea and conjunctiva. Moreover, the oral exposure can cause a disturbance in the reproductive, developmental, and neuronal systems [8]. Most toxic dyes are recalcitrant to biodegradation, causing a decrease in the efficiency of biological wastewater treatment plants. Furthermore, traditional physical–chemical methods have some operational problems such as sludge generation, membrane fouling, and phase change of the pollutants [2, 9]. To avoid these problems, the use of advanced oxidative processes (AOPs) for wastewater treatment from textile industries has been proposed. AOPs are emergent and promising processes for removal of persistent organic pollutants. The main factor in the degradation of pollutants is by the generation of highly oxidant and nonselective hydroxyl radicals ($^{\bullet}OH$) that promote the reaction of different classes of organic compounds. This technology can lead the complete mineralization or promote the formation of more biodegradable intermediates. The AOPs can be applied to a large set of different matrixes and that decontamination occurs through pollutants of degradation instead of their simple phase transfer. These methodologies become even more attractive when they use the sunlight as the source of energy [10, 11]. Although different advanced oxidation processes use several different reaction systems, all of them have the same chemical characteristic, i.e., the production and use of $^{\bullet}OH$ [12–14].

Among AOPs, heterogeneous photocatalysis has been very attractive because the use of sunlight activated the process, allowing energy economy [15]. Heterogeneous photocatalysis produces oxidizing species able to promote degradation of organic pollutants through semiconductor as the catalyst. Typically, TiO_2, ZnO, CdS, and ZnS semiconductors are employed in photocatalysis due to the electronic structure. It has a fully occupied valence band (VB) and an empty conduction band (CB). In this way, excited electrons can be transferred to chemicals into the semiconductor particle environment, and at the same time, the catalyst accepts electrons of oxidized species [12, 13]. Photocatalysis action mechanism can be visualized in Figure 2.

The semiconductor (TiO_2) absorbs photons equal or higher than that of the band gap to promote an electron from the VB to the CB. Consequently, an electron/hole pair is formed as described by the following set of equations:

$$TiO_2 + hu \rightarrow h^+_{VB} + e^-_{CB} \tag{1}$$

The hole produced in the VB can oxidize the water presents in the medium producing $^{\bullet}OH$ and oxidize hydroxide ions or the substrate itself, according to Figure 2.

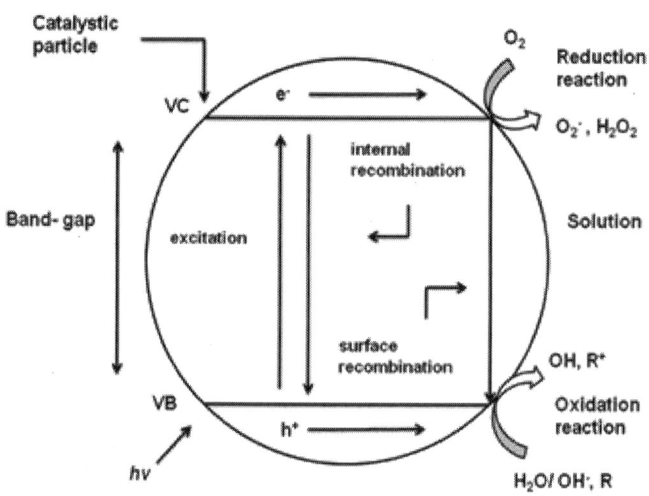

Figure 2. Mechanism of semiconductor (TiO_2) particle surface.

$$TiO_2\left(h^+_{VB}\right) + H_2O_{adsorv} \rightarrow TiO_2 + {}^{\bullet}OH_{adsorv} + H^+ \tag{2}$$

$$TiO_2\left(h^+_{VB}\right) + OH^-_{adsorv} \rightarrow TiO_2 + {}^{\bullet}OH_{adsorv} \tag{3}$$

$$TiO_2\left(h^+{}_{VB}\right) + RX_{adsorv} \rightarrow TiO_2 + RX\bullet^+{}_{adsorv} \tag{4}$$

Moreover, the electrons promoted to the CB are also able to reduce the oxygen available for superoxide radicals. Thus, the presence of oxygen is essential in all oxidative processes:

$$TiO_2\left(e^-{}_{CB}\right) + O_2 \rightarrow TiO_2 + O_2\bullet^- \tag{5}$$

Titanium dioxide is a well-known photocatalyst mostly used in photoreactions for wastewater treatment [16]. Fujishima and Honda [17] studied the heterogeneous photocatalysis of water extensively by TiO_2. As a consequence, several studies have reported the use of titanium dioxide as process able to degrade all persistent pollutants [18–23] and wastewater textile dyes from industries [24, 25]. The TiO_2 has low cost and toxicity, high photochemical reactivity, and non-specific oxidative attack. In this way, it can promote the degradation of organic compounds with little change of operational parameters [26]. TiO_2 has significant advantages for environmental application at the fact converted persistent organic molecules to safe oxidation products such CO_2 and H_2O [27]. Additionally, it can be used as an antibacterial agent due to its strong oxidation activity and hydrophilicity [28].

To perform a heterogeneous photocatalytic reaction is necessary to use semiconductors with the adequate "band gap" to be activated by solar energy. TiO_2 has a high band gap, of 3.2 eV, being consequently activated only by radiation below 380 nm. On the other hand, metal oxides, such as TiO_2, are resistant to photocorrosion with an adequate application on photocatalysis [28].

The decolorization of a model water effluent containing IC dye mediated by TiO_2 indicated that IC photodegradation depends on various parameters, e.g., the initial concentration of the dye, the amount of TiO_2, pH of the solution, the presence of inorganic anions, temperature, and the addition of different concentrations of hydrogen peroxide. Furthermore, the efficiency of the photocatalytic process strongly depends on the geometry of the photoreactor, which should enable all photocatalyst particles to be fully illuminated. Different photoreactors under artificial and solar irradiation were used, and their efficiency tested on the photodegradation of IC dye. On the other hand, photocatalytic degradation may generate photoproducts more toxic than their parent compounds. Thus, it is important to assess the toxicity of the resultant solution after treatment to determine potential threats to biodiversity of the treated waste to be released into the environment.

Although most of the experiments with IC reported in the literature were performed with the photocatalysts dispersed in water to enable the post-treatment photocatalysts removal, it is most important to use an immobilized catalyst. This chapter makes a comprehensive approach to the different results on the remediation of model effluents containing IC dye.

2. Heterogeneous photocatalysis degradation of Indigo carmine dye

2.1. Degradation of Indigo carmine dye under different geometry reactors

Heterogeneous photocatalysis processes require the maximum utilization of photons generated by artificial light or solar irradiation. The photochemical solar technology included the geometry design reactors for efficient solar photon collections to promote the photodegradation of organic pollutants presents on wastewater effluents [6]. The degradation of the IC dye was studied under different irradiation source and geometry reactors. Figure 3 shows the reactors that have been used to study the degradation at a laboratory bench top scale. First, Figure 3A shows a batch magnetically stirred reactor, irradiated with a high pressure of 125 W mercury vapor lamp (Reactor 1). Due to lamp geometry, a single point of stirring is applied. Second, Figure 3B shows a batch magnetically stirred with irradiation being ensured by four parallel 20 W daylight lamps; as light distribution is always identical below the lamps, multipoint stirring can be used (Reactor 2). The reactor presented on Figure 3C consists of a glass tubular continuous-flow reactor illuminated by one 20 W daylight lamp, fitted inside the tubular reactor (Reactor 3). The dye solution is pumped through this reactor, between lamp and inside's reactor wall, circulating to/from a storage beaker.

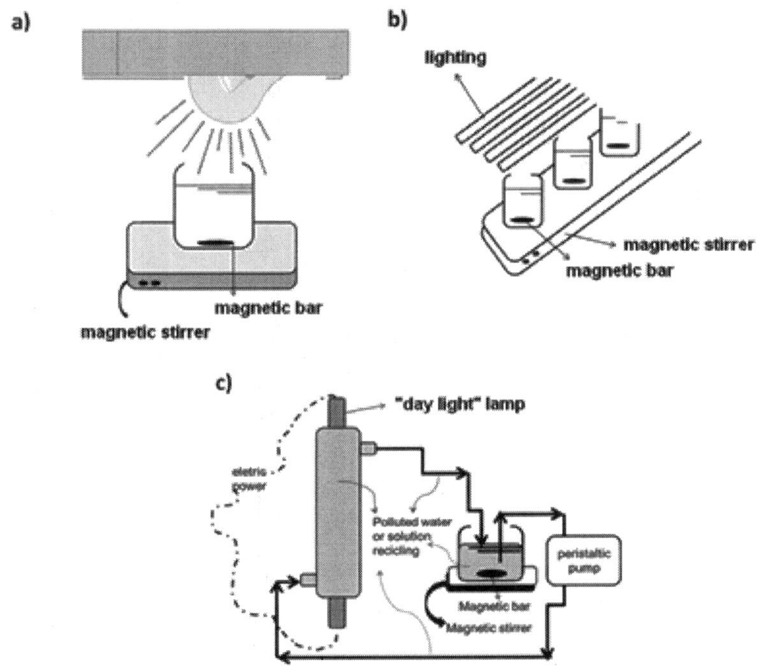

Figure 3. Reactors used on photocatalytic degradation of Indigo carmine dye in water [29].

In all cases, the efficiency of photocatalytic degradation of IC was directly related to the amount of photocatalyst. The optimum concentration of TiO_2 (i.e., the minimum photocatalyst concentration enabling the highest photodegradation rate) depended on the geometry of the photoreactor that should enable all photocatalyst particles to be fully illuminated. For improvement of the photocatalysis efficiency, especially under solar irradiation, an equipment that makes a more efficient collection of photons could be applied. This equipment, already a pilot plant reactor, is a solar collector coupled to the tubular reactor where degradation itself takes place, and it usually represents the largest source of operating costs of a photocatalysis unit for treatment of effluents. This reactor, whose simplified diagram is presented in Figure 4, is a tubular reactor with compound parabolic solar concentration. These reactors are static parabolic collectors with a parabolic reflective surface that have their axis (where sunlight concentrates the most) a tubular reactor, where wastewater to be remediated flows through as shown in Figure 4. They had demonstrated to provide an excellent efficiency in the treatment of low pollutant's concentration effluents [29].

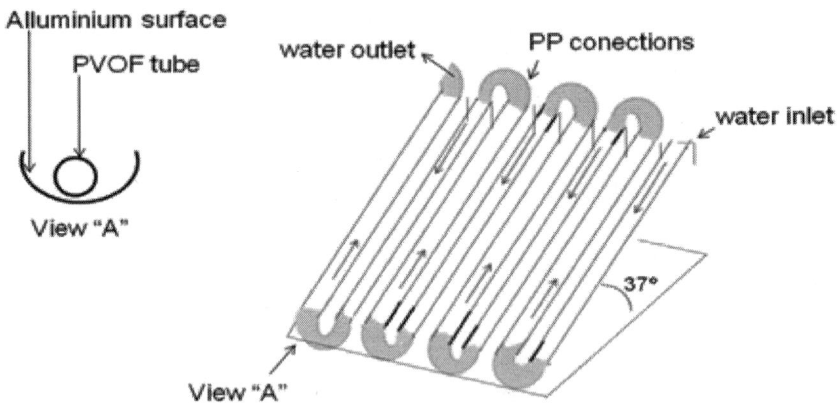

Figure 4. Simplified diagram of a compound parabolic collecting (CPC) reactor (CPC) [29].

Reactor 1 demonstrated the best results in photocatalytic degradation for IC. Photocatalysis efficiency at 96% and 92% was achieved in 30 minutes for concentrations of 1 g L^{-1} and 1×10^{-1} g L^{-1} of TiO_2, respectively. On the other hand, the photodegradation on Reactors 2 and 3 was very slower with 100% of IC degradation at 1440 minutes of irradiation time under the same TiO_2 concentrations [29]. The results obtained for Reactor 1 were very similar to the ones obtained under sunlight irradiation during summer because the photon flux used in both processes was similar. It is possible to replace artificial light source by natural solar light irradiation with the same efficiency. Furthermore, experiments carried out in winter months also demonstrated reasonable efficiencies. The photolysis of the dye was negligible for the compound parabolic reactor (CPC) like for the experiments in batch lab reactors. On the other hand, in distilled water, its photodegradation was observed to be complete for an accumulated UV energy of 15 kJ L^{-1}, correspondingly approximately to only 12 minutes of irradiation time [29].

The absorbance of the IC dye at 610 nm decreased gradually with prolonged light exposure due to an increase in decolorization and light-induced degradation. Figure 5 shows the fast decolorization of 610 nm and also the changes of the spectra in the UV region. The decolorization of IC solutions is associated with the cleavage of double-bond carbon (–C=C–), characteristic of indigoid dye molecules (Figure 1) [30]. Absorption in the UV region can be assigned to the aromatic rings and exhibited peaks at 286 and 250 nm [31]. The intermediates may have been formed as demonstrated the changes of indigo dye UV–visible spectra. Lower molecular weight (MW) organic compounds or carbon dioxide probably is the most intermediates formed by oxidation of original IC structure [32].

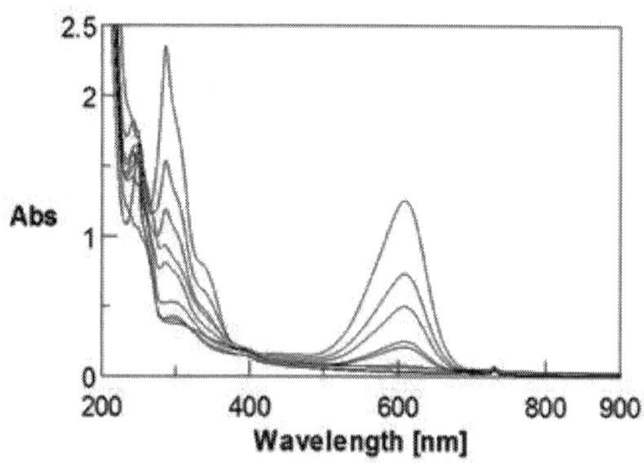

Figure 5. Time dependent UV–visible spectrum of Indigo carmine. Initial concentration of IC: 30 mg L^{-1}; dosage of TiO_2: $1{\times}10^{-2}$ g L^{-1}. Spectra from top to bottom correspond to irradiation times of 0, 15, 30, 45, 60, 90, 120, 180, and 300 min, respectively. Experiments performed with Reactor 1, in Figure 3A [29].

The solar irradiation batch lab experiments were very helpful to establish the best conditions for different geometries and light source for the photodegradation of IC dye. It facilitates the correspondence between various reactors with artificial irradiation and solar irradiation on the photodegradation of IC dye [29]. The summarized results indicate the feasibility of solar photocatalysis with TiO_2 to the treatment of IC effluents from a textile industry, mainly in regions with available sunlight throughout the year. Moreover, titanium dioxide application to be activated by sunlight is compatible with the green chemistry principles [32].

2.2. Influence of different parameters on the photodegradation of Indigo carmine dye

2.2.1. Effect of catalyst amount

The effect of the TiO_2 amount on the photocatalytic degradation of IC was evaluated. Moreover, the significance of adsorption on the catalyst surface should also be assessed from results obtained in the absence of light. The IC adsorption on TiO_2 was found to be about 10% after 90 minutes of contact, and adsorption/desorption equilibrium time was 30 minutes in the dark. The color of indigoids dyes is influenced by the presence of associated chromophores and auxochromes groups. IC can be oxidized by positive hole or •OH or reduced by electrons in the CB where all processes were leading to the decrease in the color of water [7].

The photocatalysis efficiency is apparently directly proportional to the amount of photocatalyst used, according to Figure 6. These results can be rationalized regarding an availability of active sites on TiO_2 surface and on the light penetration for activation of TiO_2 suspensions [24]. Moreover, in suspensions containing 1 g L^{-1} of TiO_2 (first-order kinetic = 0.8442 min^{-1}), the depth of light penetration is considerably smaller than in those containing only 0.1 g L^{-1} of TiO_2 (first-order kinetic = 0.9002 min^{-1}). However, the availability of active sites is much higher. Additionally, agglomeration and sedimentation of TiO_2 particles also occur in suspensions containing a high concentration of TiO_2 [33]. In this way, the optimum amount of TiO_2 has to be determined for each solution to be treated to avoid the unnecessary use of a catalyst in excess.

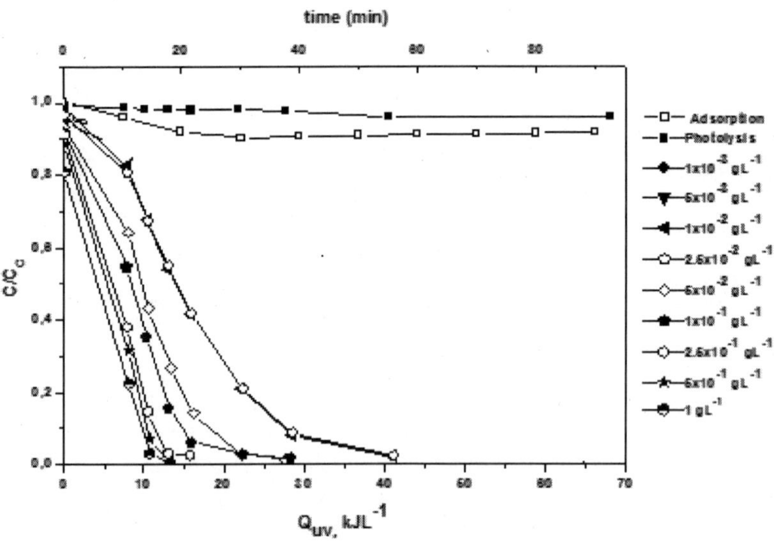

Figure 6. Effect of TiO_2 suspension concentration on the photocatalytic degradation of 30 mg L^{-1} of IC [34].

2.2.2. *Effect of initial dye concentration*

The photocatalytic degradation of the dye decreased with increase in its concentration in the sample solution. The reduction in the photodegradation rate constant can be attributed to adsorption of dye molecules on the catalyst surface and consequent decrease on the generation of •OH radicals because the active sites were occupied by dye cations [35]. Also, a significant amount of light may be absorbed by the indigo dye rather than TiO_2. Probably reducing the efficiency of the catalytic reaction, the concentration of oxidant species decreases [36]. Another possible cause of the decline of decolorization is the competition between intermediate products formed in photocatalytic processes for the limited adsorption and catalytic site on the surface of TiO_2 [37].

2.2.3. *Effect of inorganic ions*

Several anions commonly used in dye-containing industrial wastewater such as Cl^-, HCO_3^-, SO_4^{-2}, and HPO_4^{-2} should be tested. Dissolved inorganic ions may compete for the active sites on the TiO_2 surface or deactivate the photocatalyst and, subsequently, decrease the degradation efficiency [38]. In the same approach, Chen et al. [39] found that the addition of H_2PO_4 and HCO_3 significantly inhibited the degradation of Acid Orange 7 in the TiO_2 system.

For IC photodegradation, the inhibition of decolorization is exhibited:

$$HCO_3^- < Cl^- < HPO_4^{-2} < SO_4^{-2} \tag{6}$$

Inhibition effect of anions can be explained as the reaction of positive holes (h_{vb}^+) and resulting from the high reactivity and non-selectivity of •OH toward non-target compounds present in the water matrix. The HCO_3^- and Cl^- ions were with less inhibition effect on IC decolorization. In TiO_2/UV system, HCO_3^- can trap •OH to produce $CO_3^{\bullet -}$, which is less reactive [40]. This reaction appears to be of minor importance on the photodegradation of the IC. Additionally, in the case of Cl^- under neutral or alkaline conditions, the addition of Cl^- ion did not influence the reaction [41]. On the other hand, the SO_4^{-2} ions demonstrated more inhibition on the decolorization rate because it is possible for a high competitive adsorption of the dye on the TiO_2 surface, and they can trap both positive holes (h^+) and •OH [41].

2.2.4. *Effect of temperature*

The IC photodegradation is temperature dependent, and it decreases with the rise of solution temperature.

It is known that an increase in temperature can affect the efficiency of e^-/h^+ recombination and adsorption/desorption processes of dye molecules on the TiO_2 photocatalyst surface [42]. Some of the most important surface phenomena are dye molecule aggregation, tautomerization, and geometric (*cis–trans*) isomerization, and all those processes can be affected by temperature variation. The increase in solution temperature causes disaggregation of the dye molecules [24].

Habib et al. [24] considered MW and anion site (sulfate and a carboxylic group), which can interact with molecules by ion–dipole interactions. According to these authors, the dye has low MW and less anionic showed a significant variation under different temperatures. Consequently, the change of the temperature of the solution has a significant effect on the effective collisions between dyes and the TiO_2 photocatalyst. In this case, the IC molecules possess a comparatively low MW (466.36 g mol^{-1}) and only two anion sites (sulfate groups). Therefore, the variation of the temperature should also affect its photodegradation.

2.2.5. *Effect of hydrogen peroxide addition*

The principal problem found in most photocatalysis processes using TiO_2 is the undesired electron/hole recombination, which represents the major energy-wasting step, thus restricting the feasible quantum yield of the photodegradation process. Hydrogen peroxide is an electron donor favoring the photocatalytic process inhibiting electron–hole recombination [43]. In this sense, the effect of H_2O_2 on the photocatalytic degradation of IC is examined. It was noted that when the hydrogen peroxide concentration increases, the photodegradation suffers an initial increase up to H_2O_2 0.022M and decrease at higher concentrations. Hydrogen peroxide at low concentration acts mainly as a source of $^{\bullet}OH$ and as an electron scavenger inhibiting the electron–hole recombination (Eq. 7) [44].

$$H_2O_2 + e^-_{CB} \rightarrow OH\bullet + OH^- \tag{7}$$

However, at higher concentrations, H_2O_2 reacts with $^{\bullet}OH$ and acts itself as a scavenger of the photoproduced holes. The H_2O_2 excess acts itself as a scavenger of the photoproduced holes. In this way, they behave like the self-quenching process of $^{\bullet}OH$ to form hydroperoxyl radicals ($OOH^{\bullet}$) (Eq. 8), where oxidation potential is much lower than that of $^{\bullet}OH$ [45], leading to a decrease in the photocatalytic efficiency.

$$H_2O_2 + {}^{\bullet}OH \rightarrow H_2O + {}^{\bullet}OOH \tag{8}$$

The optimum dosage of H_2O_2 is variable and has been reported that it was dependent on the initial dye concentration.

2.2.6. *Effect of Initial pH*

The effect of pH changes on the photodegradation rate is studied in the range of pH 2–11. The photocatalytic reaction occurs on the surface of the catalyst and is dependent on TiO_2 surface charge. In this way, the adsorptive properties of TiO_2 particles depended strongly on the solution pH [46]. The degradation of IC is faster in acid solutions (i.e., pH ranges from 2 to 5). At neutral and basic medium, the rate of dye degradation is slow, nevertheless in accumulated energy of Q_{uv} 70 kJ L^{-1}, all IC solutions are degraded. This effect can be explained by the surface charge density of TiO_2. The point of zero charge (pzc) of TiO_2 is at pH = 6.8. Thus, the TiO_2 surface is fully protonated in medium acidic solution and negatively charged under alkaline conditions (Eqs. 9 and 10) [47]:

$$pH < pzc: \Leftrightarrow TiOH + H^+TiOH_2^+ \tag{9}$$

$$pH < pzc: \Leftrightarrow TiOH + OH^- \ TiO^- + H_2O \tag{10}$$

Considering the IC structure has sulfuric groups, which are negatively charged, at pH < 5.0, the positive charge through protonation (Eq. 9) on the photocatalyst surface promotes active interaction of a dye onto the catalyst surface and improves the photocatalytic degradation. On the other hand, for the basic solutions (pH > pzc), the surface of the catalyst is negatively charged through the proton abstraction by hydroxide ion (Eq. 10). Consequently, repulsions between a negative-charged surface of the catalyst and anionic dye fragments retard the surface adsorption, resulting in a low-photodegradation activity [48].

2.2.7. *Effect of water matrix*

In distilled water IC degradation is observed to be complete for an accumulated UV energy of 15 kJ L^{-1}, correspondingly ~12 minutes of irradiation time. However, for complex matrices of water like freshwater and simulated municipal wastewater treatment plant (MWWTP) secondary effluent, the degradation of the dye is slower. The freshwater and simulated MWWTP secondary effluent required ~25 kJ L^{-1} for complete photodegradation. When a real MWWTP secondary effluent was carried out, the complete IC photodegradation occurred at accumulated energy around 33 kJ L^{-1}. It is demonstrated that as the matrix more complex, the degradation rate of organic compounds is slower. This fact can be explained the presence of carbonate species on real wastewater that act as scavengers of the $^{\bullet}OH$ generated on photocatalysis [49], as showed in Figure 7. Table 1 exhibited a high concentration of inorganic carbon in the real effluent, which is widely found in real wastewater [50].

Type of water	Inorg. Carbon (ppm)	TOC (ppm)	COD (ppm)	pH	Conduc. (μs cm^{-1})	Ionic species (mM)							
						Na^{+}	Ca^{+2}	Mg^{+2}	K^{+}	NH^{+4}	PO_4^{-3}	Cl^{-}	SO_4^{-2}
Fresh water	13.89	3.40	11.6	7.4	206	0.76	0.36	0.44	0.1	–	–	0.09	0.04
Synthetic MWWTP secondary effluent	9.98	17.76	57.59	8.0	261	1.27	0.36	0.45	0.17	0.35	0.01	0.04	0.93
Real MWWTP secondary effluent	69.92	26.9	81.2	8.3	1504	8.2	1.5	1.3	0.63	2.96	0.05	9.94	1.02

Table 1. Characteristics physical and chemical of different water matrices [29]

The total degradation of organic dyes leads to the conversion of organic carbon into gaseous CO_2, whereas nitrogen and sulfur heteroatoms are converted into inorganic ions, such as nitrate or ammonium and sulfate ions, respectively. In distilled water, the mineralization of the IC dye was completed around 90 kJ L^{-1} of accumulated energy. When complex matrices

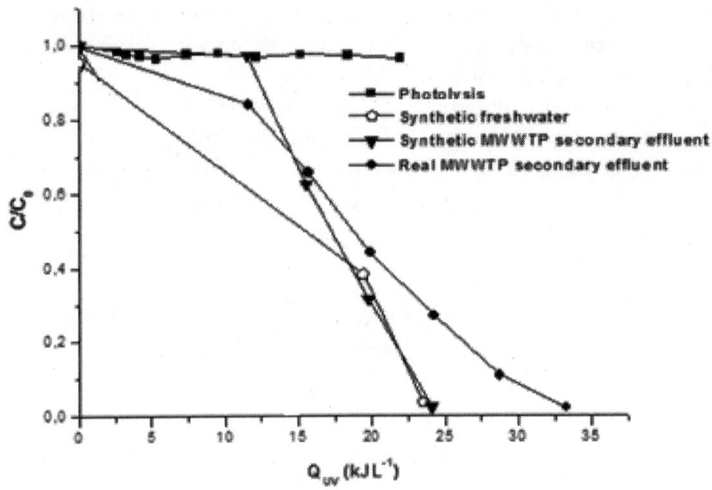

Figure 7. Photodegradation of Indigo carmine for different type of water mediated by 0.1 g L^{-1} of TiO_2 suspensions [29].

were tested, the mineralization was not complete. However, considering the theoretic TOC of the IC (12 mg L^{-1}) and initial TOC of the matrices (see Table 1), the dye was totally mineralized even in the presence of scavenger species [29].

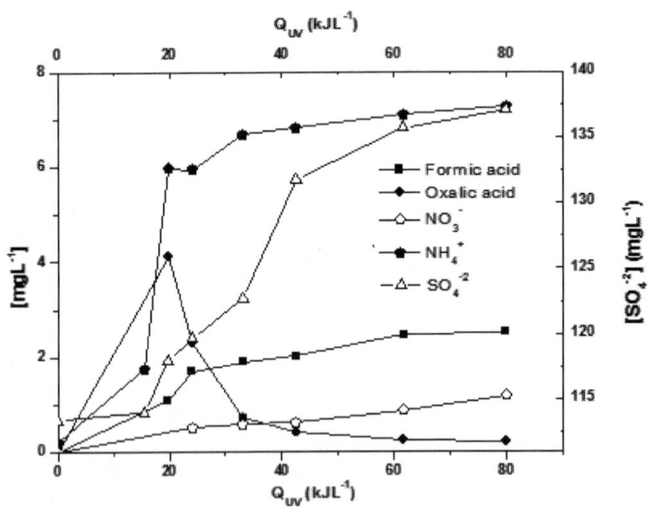

Figure 8. Ions and carboxylic acid concentrations formed during photodegradation of Indigo carmine [29].

The structure of IC dye has two sulfonic groups attached to two aromatic rings, and these results indicate that SO_4^{-2} ions are formed during the process. However, the sulfate ion concentration is lower than expected from theory stoichiometry, because by adsorption of SO_4^{-2} at the surface of titanium dioxide [51]. The evolution of NH_4^+ suggests that this ion is the primary N-containing mineralization product. It indicates its origin as first products resulted from the initial attack on the carbon-to-carbon double bond of IC. The formic and oxalic acids remain for the UV-accumulated energy of 80 kJ L^{-1} indicating the evaluation of ecotoxicology tests, according to Figure 8.

2.2.8. Recycling of TiO_2

One of today's main industrial wastewater treatment strategies is focused on the development of green technologies and management practices for environmental benefit. To attend this "new"concept, the recycling of the photocatalyst should be performed. In this study, the TiO_2 catalyst was recycled for consecutive reuse on this procedure up to eight times [34].

According to the results (Figure 9), the effectiveness of the TiO_2 decreased from 98% (first cycle) to 80% (fifth cycle) and subsequently to 50% (sixth cycle onward). However, the rate of degradation was kept significant even after eight cycles of TiO_2 reuse. The effectiveness of complete separation of photocatalysts from treated water is a critical step required to maintain a satisfactory degradation [52]. Moreover, agglomeration and sedimentation of IC around TiO_2 particles after each cycle of photocatalytic degradation are a possible cause of the observed decrease in its efficiency [53]. This study further shows that the reuse of the TiO_2 presents a promising photocatalytic performance with little variation of decay rate after eight consecutive usages and also high photochemical stability.

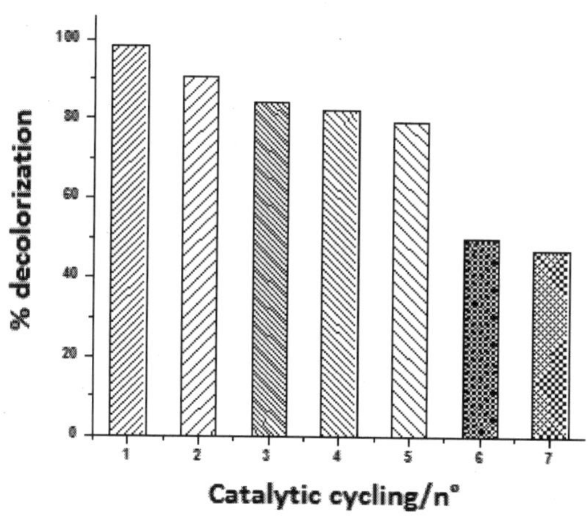

Figure 9. Recycling and reuse of TiO_2 on the photocatalytic degradation of Indigo carmine for an accumulated energy, Q_{uv}, of 15 kJ L^{-1} [34].

2.3. Supported TiO_2 on photodegradation of Indigo carmine dye

In the large-scale applications, the use of TiO_2 suspensions requires the separation and recycling of TiO_2 particles, mainly of nanometric dimension, from treated wastewater before discharge into the water bodies. This fact can be a great drawback for the application of this treatment once it is a time-consuming and an expensive process. Alternatively, the catalyst may be immobilized on a suitable solid inert material, which eliminates the need for catalyst removal step [1] and permits its reuse for several times.

On another study [29], the solar CPC photocatalytic degradation of IC using TiO_2 slurry for a treatment of real MWWTP secondary effluent demonstrated the greater efficiency of this procedure than with supported TiO_2. Probably, this indicates that the catalyst coated on glass spheres is not fully illuminated. Indeed, there are large amounts of TiO_2 particles inside the CPC tube, and a considerable amount of TiO_2 supported on glass spheres having some sites not activated for photocatalysis and lower surface area of the catalyst. However, supported TiO_2 has the enormous advantage of eliminating the catalyst removal step and thus reducing the costs of treatment considerably.

It should be emphasized that the decrease in the color of the IC solutions not provide complete data on the IC dye degradation. The TOC decrease suggests that during the irradiation processes of supported TiO_2, a large number of low MW compounds are formed. Furthermore, hydroxylation of aromatic reaction products leads to cleavage of the aromatic ring, resulting in the formation of oxygen-containing aliphatic compounds [31]. On the other hand, after the fading stage, a breakdown of carbon-to-carbon double bond of IC may form inorganic ions. Formate, acetate, and oxalate are detected during degradation in real MWWTP secondary effluent containing IC as shown in Figure 10.

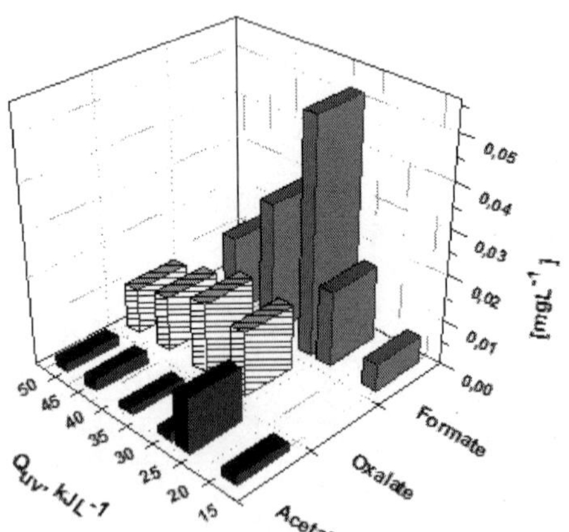

Figure 10. Evaluation of the concentrations of carboxylic acids followed by ion chromatography; formed during solar CPC photodegradation of Indigo carmine with supported TiO_2 in real MWWTP secondary effluent [34].

2.4. Decolorization of Indigo carmine dye using activated carbon/TiO_2/UV

First, the use of activated carbon (AC) is an efficient water and wastewater treatment; the treatment is based on the use of adsorbent substrates and has many applications on textile dye's wastewater treatments [54]. AC is probably the most versatile adsorbent because of its large surface area, polymodal porous structure, high adsorption capacity, and variable surface chemical composition. Furthermore, what makes ACs attractive to (textile) wastewater treatment is the possibility of tailoring their physical and/or chemical properties to optimize their performance on top of its, already powerful, strong hydrophobic and amorphous character [55]. The synergic role of AC with TiO_2 is also a parameter to investigate once it opens the opportunity to combine adsorption and photocatalytic remediation. In this way, the decolorization of the model effluent containing indigo dye is revised using AC in the dark and under irradiation and AC/TiO_2/UV.

The AC is used in two different situations. First, the AC in various concentrations is add in the solution of IC dye and kept in the dark. Furthermore, AC is submitted to the same conditions but kept under artificial irradiation during the all-time experiment. Similar decolorization rates are obtained when comparing experiments with different amounts of AC in the dark. Only in high concentrations, AC is able to remove the dye, but in this case, the determinant removal mechanism is adsorption of the dye in AC microporous structure. On the other hand, AC is not able to produce strong photocatalytic activity and had only adsorptive properties with an adsorption capacity of 28.5 mg IC per gram of carbon. The decolorization of AC/TiO_2/UV following the same profile of TiO_2/UV, but the constant K in TiO_2/UV was by itself more efficiency when compared with AC/TiO_2/UV. TiO_2 activity decreased in the presence of AC not only because AC can absorb light—i.e., by reducing the light flux in the sample—but also because AC can adsorb TiO_2, reducing the amount of photocatalyst available.

2.5. Ecotoxicological assessment

Photocatalytic degradation may generate toxic photoproducts. Thus, it is important to assess the toxicity of the solution after treatment. The ecotoxicological tests of IC and its photoproducts obtained by photocatalytic remediation treatment were evaluated. Two essays, two aquatic organisms, and one terrestrial organism were used. Aquatic organism represented by algae *Pseudokirchneriella subcapitata* (Chlorophyceae), a primary consumer *Daphnia similis* (Cladocera), and earthworm *Eisenia andrei* as terrestrial organism [29, 56, 57].

For all organisms, ecotoxicity tests are performed comparing the effects of solutions containing IC before and after photocatalytic treatment with TiO_2. Chronic toxicity tests with *P. subcapitata* indicated no significant toxic effect for any tested samples (Table 2), but sample containing IC, the sample with photoproducts in pH 7 and sample with TiO_2 filtered strongly stimulated algal growth indicating nutritional effects. Thus, the release of IC dye or its photoproducts into aquatic ecosystems may be expected to cause algal growth.

The species *D. similis* had a different response. Acute toxicity tests showed that IC dye caused a low toxicity, but photoproducts are highly toxic (Table 2). Photoproducts in pH 4 and 7, respectively, caused a mortality of 100%. According to Vautier et al. [7], photocatalysis of IC

Samples	*P. subcapitata* chronic test		*D. similis* acute test	
	Mean ± SD (#cells ml^{-1})	**Observed Response**	**Mortality (%)**	**pH**
Blank	119± 5	None	0	7.8
Indigo carmine only	315± 99	164% growth	20	7.1
Photoproducts generated by TiO_2 photocatalysis (pH 4)	113± 20	5% inhibition	100	4.2
Photoproducts generated by TiO_2 photocatalysis (pH 7)	395± 48	231% growth	100	7.0
Indigo carmine + TiO_2 - without photodegradation (time 0)	135± 15	13% growth	0	7.1
TiO_2 + ultrapure water	389± 37	227% growth	20	7.2

Table 2. Number of *Pseudokirchneriella subcapitata* cells per ml after 72h exposition, and percent immobilization of *Daphnia similis* after 48h exposition [29]

produces mainly aromatic metabolites such as 2-nitrobenzaldehyde and anthranilic. Moreover, carboxylic acids fragments are also present, such as malic and tartaric acids [29]. On the other hand, studies demonstrated that in the presence of TiO_2, absorption of some toxicants can be increased [29, 58]. In this approach, it a significant challenge to complete the removal of nano-TiO_2 after releasing treated effluents to prevent its contamination of aquatic ecosystems [29].

Furthermore, terrestrial acute ecotoxicological tests with *E. andrei* earthworms are performed. The earthworms are affected by various organic and inorganic compounds, which may cause bioaccumulation, and their preliminary results serve as a rapid indicator of the toxicity of the compounds. Moreover, it can be used as a complementary test for risk assessment of polluted areas [59]. Effects of different IC concentration and its photoproducts on earthworms are studied. In all cases, no mortality is observed. No significant difference ($p > 0.05$) of a reduction in mean weight earthworms is found from the paper treated with different concentrations of IC. Toxicity tests with earthworms are also carried out for the photodegradation products of IC, and no mortality is observed after 24 h exposure to different treatments. These results suggest that the presence of IC and its photoproducts do not demonstrate an effect on the earthworms for acute contact test (24 h). However, more tests must be performed for a better understanding of the IC toxicity for *E. andrei*.

3. Conclusions

Photodegradation of IC by TiO_2 was successful to remove colour from water; nevertheless, the degradation of IC in water with powdered TiO_2 depends on various parameters. Among the systems evaluated, the Reactor 1 (125 W mercury vapour lamp) was the most efficient. Solar photocatalysis demonstrated better efficient in the summer but degraded the dye in the winter completely; then both seasons allow the solar photocatalysis efficient. CPC pilot plant photocatalysis simulated real situations of environmental remediation, reducing the duration and costs of the treatment. Moreover, a TiO_2 catalyst supported on glass spheres proved to have high efficiency to remove IC in different water matrices even in the presence of various ions that acted as scavengers. Ecotoxicological tests revealed that photoproducts generated on photocatalysis promoted different biological responses to both tested organisms as growth effect on the algae and toxicity higher for *D. similis*. These results show the importance of photoproducts toxicity evaluation and the need for a complete removal process for TiO_2 before its release in the environment.

References

[1] Barka N, Assabbane A, Nounah A, Aîlchou Y. Photocatalytic degradation of Indigo carmine in aqueous solution by TiO_2-coated non-woven fibres. J Hazard Mater. 2008;152:1054–59. DOI: 10.1016/j.jhazmat.2007.07.080.

[2] Zainal Z, Hui LK, Hussein MZ, Taufiq-Yap YH, Abdullah AH, Ramli I. Removal of dyes using immobilized titanium dioxide illuminated by fluorescent lamps. J Hazard Mater. 2005;125:113–20. DOI: 10.1016/j.jhazmat.2005.05.013.

[3] Behnajaday MA, Modirhahla N, Daneshvar N, Rabban M. Photocatalytic degradation of an azo dye in a tubular continuous-flow photoreactor with immobilized TiO_2 on glass plates. Chem Eng J. 2007;127:167–76. DOI: 10.1016/j.cej.2006.09.013.

[4] Robinson T, McMullan G, Marchant R, Nigam P. Remediation of dyes in textile effluent: a critical review on current treatment technologies with a proposed alternative. Bioresour Technol. 2001;77:247–55. DOI: 10.1016/S0960-8524(00)00080-8.

[5] Andreotti A, Bonaduce L, Colombini MP, Ribechini E. Characterisation of natural indigo and shellfish purple by mass spectrometric techniques. Rapid Commun Mass Spectrom. 2004;18:1213–20. DOI: 10.1002/rcm.1464.

[6] Oliveira AS, Saggioro EM, Barbosa NR, Mazzei A, Ferreira LFV, Moreira JC. Surface photocatalysis: a study of the thickness of TiO_2 layers on the photocatalytic decomposition of soluble Indigo Blue dye. Rev Chim. 2011;62:462–68.

[7] Vautier M, Guillard C, Herrmann J. Photocatalytic degradation of dyes in water: case study of Indigo carmine. J Catal. 2001;201:46–59. DOI: 10.1006/jcat.2001.3232.

[8] Jenkins CL. Textile dyes are potential hazards. Arch Environ Health. 1978;40:7–12.

[9] Sanromán MA, Pazos M, Ricart MT, Cameselle C. Electrochemical decolourisation of structurally different dyes. Chemosphere. 2004;57:233–39. DOI: 10.1016/j.chemosphere.2004.06.019.

[10] Sano T, Puzenat E, Guillard C, Geantet C, Matsuzawa S. Degradation of C_2H_2 with modified-TiO_2 photocatalysts under visible light irradiation. Journal of Molecular Catalysis A: Chemical. 2008;284:127–133. DOI: 10.1016/j.molcata.2008.01.014.

[11] Khataee V, Vatanpour V, Amani AR. Decolorization of C.I. acid blue 9 solution by UV/nano-TiO_2, Fenton, Fenton-like, electro-Fenton and electrocoagulation processes: a comparative study. Journal of Hazardous Materials. 2009;161:1225–1233. DOI: 10.1016/j.jhazmat.2008.04.075.

[12] Eckenfelder WW. Industrial Water Pollution Control. 3rd ed. McGrawHill; 2000. 600 p. ISBN: 978-0070393646.

[13] Metcalf & Eddy. Wastewater Engineering – Treatment and Reuse. 4rd ed. McGraw-Hill; 2003. 1848 p. ISBN: 0-07-124140X.

[14] Linsebigler AL, Lu G, Yates JT. Photocatalysis on TiO_2 surfaces: principles, mechanisms and selected rules. Chemical Review. 1995;95:735–768.

[15] Zhao J, Wu T, Wu K, Oikawa K, Hidaka H, Serpone N. Photoassisted degradation of dye pollutants. 3. Degradation of the cationic dye rhodamine B in aqueous anionic surfactant/TiO_2 dispersions under visible light irradiation: evidence for the need of substrate adsorption on TiO_2 particles. Environmental Science & Technology. 1998;32:2394–2400. DOI: 10.1021/es9707926.

[16] Fujishima A, Rao TN, Tryk DA. Titanium dioxide photocatalysis. Journal of Photochemistry and Photobiology C: Photochemistry Reviews. 2000;1:1–21.

[17] Fujishima A, Honda K. Electrochemical photolysis of water at a semiconductor electrode. Nature. 1972;238:37–8. DOI: 10.1038/238037a0.

[18] Mao K, Li Y, Zhang H, Zhang W, Yan W. Photocatalytical degradation of 17-ethinylestradiol and inactivation of *Escherichia coli* using Ag-modified TiO_2 nanotube arrays. Clean – Soil Air Water. 2013;41:455–462. DOI: 10.1002/clen.201100698.

[19] Ghosh JP, Achari G, Langford CP. Reductive dechlorination of PCBs using photocatalyzed UV light. Clean – Soil Air Water. 2012;40:455–460. DOI: 10.1002/clen.201100186.

[20] Beduk F, Aydin ME, Ozcan S. Degradation of malathion and parathion by ozonation, photolytic ozonation and heterogeneous catalytic ozonation processes. Clean – Soil Air Water. 2012;40:179–187. DOI: 10.1002/clen.201100063.

[21] Martins AF, Mayer F, Confortin EC, Frank CS. a study of photocatalytical processes involving the degradation of the organic load and amoxicillin in hospital wastewater. Clean – Soil Air Water 2009;37:365–371. DOI: 10.1002/clen.200800022.

[22] Kist LT, Albrecht C, Machado EL. Hospital laundry wastewater disinfection with catalytic photoozonation. Clean – Soil Air Water. 2008;36:775–780. DOI: 10.1002/clen.200700175.

[23] Oliveira AS, Maia CG, Brito P, Boscencu R, Socoteanu R, Ilie M, Ferreira LFV. Photodegradation of photodynamic therapy agents in aqueous TiO_2 suspensions. Sustainable Develop Plan VI. 2013;173:359–369.

[24] Habibi MH, Hassanzadeh A, Mahdavi S. The effect of operational parameters on the photocatalytical degradation of three textile azo dyes in aqueous TiO_2 suspensions. J Photochem Photobiol A Chem. 2005;172:89–96. DOI: 10.1016/j.jphotochem.2004.11.009.

[25] Neamatu M, Simiriceanu I, Yediler A, Kettrup A. Kinetics of decolorization and mineralization of reactive azo dyes in aquous solution by the UV/H_2O_2 oxidation. Dyes Pigm. 2002;53:93–99. DOI: 10.1016/S0143-7208(02)00012-8.

[26] Chen C, Wang Z, Ruan S, Zou B, Zhao M, Wu F. Photocatalytic degradation of C.I. Acid Orange 52 in the presence of Zn-doped TiO_2 prepared by a stearic acid gel method. Dyes and Pigments. 2008;77:204–209. DOI: 10.1016/j.dyepig.2007.05.003.

[27] Hoffman MR, Martin ST, Choi WY, Bahnemann DW. Environmental applications of semiconductor photocatalysis. Chemical Reviews. 1995;95:69–96. DOI: 10.1021/cr00033a004.

[28] Fujishima X, Zhang CR. Titanium dioxide photocatalysis: present situation and future approaches. Comptes Rendus Chimie. 2006;9:750–760. DOI: 10.1016/j.crci.2005.02.055.

[29] Saggioro EM, Oliveira AS, Buss DF, Magalhães DP, Pavesi T, Jimenéz M, Maldonado MI, Ferreira LFV, Moreira JC. Photo-decolorization and ecotoxicological effects of solar compound parabolic collector pilot plant and artificial light photocatalysis of In-

digo carmine dye. Dyes and Pigments. 2015;113:571–580. DOI: 10.1016/j.dyepig.2014.09.029.

[30] Gemeay AH, Mansour IA, El-Sharkawy RG, Zaki AB. Kinetics and mechanism of the heterogeneous catalyzed oxidative degradation of Indigo carmine. J Mol Catal A Chem. 2003;193:109–120. DOI: 10.1016/S1381-1169(02)00477-6.

[31] Al-Ekabi H, Serpone N. Photocatalytic degradation of chlorinated phenols in aerated aqueous solutions over TiO_2 supported on a glass matrix. J Phys Chem. 1998;92:5726–5731. DOI: 10.1021/j100331a036.

[32] Velmurugan R, Swaminathan M. An efficient nanostructured ZnO for dye sensitized degradation of Reactive Red 120 dye under solar light. Sol Energ Mat Sol C. 2011;95:942–950. DOI: 10.1016/j.solmat.2010.11.029.

[33] Saggioro EM, Oliveira AS, Pavesi T, Maia CG, Ferreira LFV, Moreira JC. Use of titanium dioxide photocatalysis on the remediation of model textile wastewaters containing azo dyes. Molecules. 2011;16:10370–10386. DOI: 10.3390/molecules161210370.

[34] Saggioro EM, Oliveira AS, Jimenéz M, Maldonado MI, Correia FV, Moreira JC. Solar CPC pilot plant photocatalytic degradation of Indigo carmine dye in waters and wastewaters using supported-TiO_2: influence of photodegradation parameters. International Journal of Photoenergy. 2015; 20:1-12. DOI: 10.1155/2015/656153.

[35] Wang C, Lee C, Lyu M, Juang L. Photocatalytic degradation of C.I. Basic Violet 10 using TiO_2 catalysts supported by Y zeolite: an investigation of the effects of operational parameters. Dyes and Pigments. 2008;76:817–824. DOI: 10.1016/j.dyepig.2007.02.004.

[36] Augugliaro V, Baiocchi C, Prevot AB, García-López E, Loddo V, Malato S, Marcí G, Palmisano L, Pazzi M, Pramauro E. Azo-dyes photocatalytic degrdation in aqueous suspension of TiO_2 under solar irradiation. Chemosphere. 2003;49:1223–1230. DOI: 10.1016/S0045-6535(02)00489-7.

[37] Tanaka K, Padermpole K, Hisanaga T. Photocatalytic degradation of commercial azo dyes. Water Research. 2000;34:327–333. DOI: 10.1016/S0043-1354(99)00093-7.

[38] Konstantinou IK, Albanis TA. TiO_2-assisted photocatalytic degradation of azo dyes in aqueous solution: kinetic and mechanistic investigations. A review. Applied Catalysis B: Environmental. 2004;49:1–14. DOI: 10.1016/j.apcatb.2003.11.010.

[39] Chen X, Wang W, Xiao H, Hong C, Zhu F, Yao Y, Xue Z. Accelerated TiO_2 photocatalytic degradation of Acid Orange 7 under visible light mediated by peroxymonosulfate. Chemical Engineering Journal. 2012;193–194:290–295. DOI: 10.1016/j.cej.2012.04.033.

[40] Galindo C, Jacques P, Kalt A. Photodegradation of the aminoazobenzene acid Orange 52 by three advanced oxidation processes: UV/H_2O_2, UV/TiO_2 and Vis/TiO_2:

comparative mechanistic and kinetic investigations. Journal of Photochemistry and Photobiology A: Chemistry. 2000;130:35–47. DOI: 10.1016/S1010-6030(99)00199-9.

[41] Wang K, Zhang J, Lou L, Yang S, Chen Y. UV or visible light induced photodegradation of AO7 on TiO_2 particles: the influence of inorganic anions. Journal of Photochemistry and Photobiology A: Chemistry. 2004;165:201–207. DOI: 10.1016/j.jphotochem.2004.03.025.

[42] Daneshvar N, Rabbani M, Modirshahla N, Behnajady MA. Kinetic modeling of photocatalytic degradation of Acid Red 27 in UV/TiO_2 process. Journal of Photochemistry and Photobiology A: Chemistry. 2004;198:39–45. DOI: 10.1016/j.jphotochem.2004.05.011.

[43] Tseng D, Juang L, Huang H. Effect of oxygen and hydrogen peroxide on the photocatalytic degradation of monochlorobenzene in TiO_2 aqueous suspension. International Journal of Photoenergy. Article ID 328526, 2012. DOI: 10.1155/2012/328526.

[44] Dostanic JM, Loncarevic DR, Bankovic PT, Cvetkovic OG, Jovanovic DM, Mijin DZ. Influence of process parameters on the photodegradation of synthesized azo pyridine dye in TiO_2 water suspensions under simulated sunlight. Journal of Environmental Science and Health, Part A: Toxic/Hazardous Substances and Environmental Engineering. 2011;46:70–79. DOI: 10.1080/10934529.2011.526905.

[45] Haji S, Benstaali B, Al-Bastaki N. Degradation of methyl orange by UV/H_2O_2 advanced oxidation process. Chemical Engineering Journal. 2011;168:134–139. DOI: 10.1016/j.cej.2010.12.050.

[46] Senthilkumaar S, Porkodi K. Heterogeneous photocatalytic decomposition of Crystal Violet in UV-illuminated sol-gel derived nanocrystalline TiO_2 suspensions. Journal of Colloid and Interface Science. 2005;288:184–189. DOI: 10.1016/j.jcis.2005.02.066.

[47] Santiago DE, Dona-Rodríguez JM, Arana J, Fernández-Rodríguez C, González-Díaz O, Pérez-Pena J, Silva AMT. Optimization of the degradation of imazalil by photocatalysis: comparison between commercial and lab-made photocatalysts. Applied Catalysis B: Environmental. 2013;138–139:391–400. DOI: 10.1016/j.apcatb.2013.03.024.

[48] Mittal A, Mittal J, Kurup L. Batch and bulk removal of hazardous dye, Indigo carmine from wastewater through adsorption. Journal of Hazardous Materials. 2006;137:591–602. DOI: 10.1016/j.jhazmat.2006.02.047.

[49] Pelaez M, de la Cruz AA, O'Shea K, Falaras P, Dionysiou DD. Effects of water parameters on the degradation of microcystin-LR under visible light-activated TiO_2 photocatalyst. Water Research. 2011;45:3787–3796. DOI: 10.1016/j.watres.2011.04.036.

[50] Guohong X, Guoguang L, Dezhi S, Liqing Z. Kinetics of acetamiprid photolysis in solution. Bull Environ Contam Toxicol. 2009;82:129–132. DOI: 10.1007/s00128-008-9520-8.

[51] Herrmann JM, Guillard C, Arguello M, Agüera A, Tejedor A, Piedra L, Fernandez-Alba A. Photocatalytic degradation of pesticide pirimiphos-methyl – determination

of the reaction pathway and identification of intermediate products by various analytical methods. Catal Today. 1999;54:353–367. DOI: 10.1016/S0920-5861(99)00196-0.

[52] Peng Z, Tang H, Yao K. Recyclable TiO_2/carbon nanotube sponge nanocomposites: controllable synthesis, characterization and enhanced visible light photocatalytic property. Ceramics International. 2015;41:363–368. DOI: 10.1016/j.ceramint.2014.08.079.

[53] Lv Y, Yu L, Zhang X, Yao J, Zou R, Dai Z. P-doped TiO_2 nanoparticles film coated on ground glass substrate and the repeated photodegradation of dye under solar light irradiation. Applied Surface Science. 2011;257:5715–5719. DOI: 10.1016/j.apsusc.2011.01.082.

[54] Malik PK. Use of activated carbons prepared from sawdust and rice-husk for adsorption of acid dyes: a case study of Acid Yellow 36. Dyes and Pigments. 2003;56:239–249. DOI: 10.1016/S0143-7208(02)00159-6.

[55] Marsh H, Rodríguez-Reinoso F. Activated Carbon. 1st ed. Elsevier: Oxford; 2006. p. 322–327.

[56] Franciscon E, Zille A, Dias FG, Menezes CR, Durrant LR, Cavaco-Paulo A. Biodegradation of textile azo dyes by a facultative *Staphylococcus arlettae* strain VN-11 using a sequential microaerophilic/aerobic process. Int Biodeterior Biodegrad.2009;63:280–288. DOI: 10.1016/j.ibiod.2008.10.003.

[57] Bergsten-Torralba LR, Nishikawa MM, Baptista DF, Magalhães DP, da Silva M. Decolorization of different textile dyes by *Penicillium simplicissimum* and toxicity evaluation after fungal treatment. Braz J Microbiol. 2009;40:808–817.

[58] Zhang X, Sun H, Zhang Z, Niu Q, Chen Y, Crittenden JC. Enhanced bioaccumulation of cadmium in carp in the presence of titanium nanoparticles. Chemosphere. 2007;67:160–166. DOI: 10.1016/j.chemosphere.2006.09.003.

[59] Paoletti MG. The role of earthworms for assessment of sustainability and as bioindicators. Agriculture, Ecosystems & Environment. 1999;74:137–155. DOI: 10.1016/S0167-8809(99)00034-1.

Index

A

Abelmoschus esculentus 19
Adsorption process 11,19,22
Allergic 9
Aluminum chloride (Al2(Cl)3) 19
Aluminum sulfate (Al2(SO4)3) 11
Anaerobic biological processes 12
Anoxic systems 13
Antiscaling solution 16
Aquatic environment 12
Aquatic life 2,36,57,79

B

Biocatalysts 29
Biochemical oxygen demand (BOD5) 17
Biodegradable organic 20
Biodegradation 12
Biological decolorization 1,2,22
Biological degradation 12
Biological oxygen demand (BOD5) 8
Biological processes 12
Biological treatment 2,11,13,22,80
Biological treatment systems 13,14

C

Calcium 11
Carbon dioxide 13
Carcinogenic 9
Chemical coagulation 2
Chemical oxidation 1
Chemical oxygen demand (COD) 2
Chloride ferric 20
Coagulant agents 19
Colloidal solids 22
Colored fabric 5
Cut-off sunlight 2
Cutting-edge technologies 1

D

Decolorization 1
Digestion process 13
Digital printing 7
Dissolved organic 11
Dissolved organic carbon (DOM) 11
Drinking water 21
Dye consumption 4
Dye decolorization 29
Dye molecules 17
Dyeing process 16
Dyeing wastewaters 1

E

Electrochemical processes 1,18,19
Electrochemical techniques 11
Electrochemical treatment processes 1
Electrocoagulation 18
Electro-fenton 18
Electrolysis 18
Electron acceptor 13
Energy consumption 3,18,24,81
Energy source 17
Environmental engineers 2
Environmental friendly 13
Environmental pollution 1,2,7,22
Environmental problems 2
Environmental systems 12
Enzyme technology 29
Enzymes 29

F

Fenton process 18
Ferric sulfate (Fe2(SO4)3) 11
Fixation ratio 4
Flocculants 19
Flocculation 2

G

Global industry 3
Green technology 6
Growth system 13

H

Hazardous waste 3
Heavy metals 3,8,12,22,24,52,94
Hollow fiber nanofiltration 16
Hybrid processes 1,20
Hybrid/combined processes 2
Hydrodynamic energy 17
Hydrogen peroxide 17,18,96,102,113
Hydroxyl radicals (HO˙) 17,18

I

Immobilization 29

L

Liquid dispersions 4
Low biodegradability 2
Lysochromes 4

M

Membrane bioreactor (MBR) 14,16,22
Membrane photoreactor 21
Membrane processes 1,14,17,22
Membrane separation 2
Membrane separation processes 1
Membrane surface 16
Membrane systems 22
Membrane technologies 16
Microfiltration 16
Microorganism 13
Mixed microbial populations 14
Molecular free oxygen 13

N

Naphthol dyes 4
Natural polymers 19
Nitrogen 16
Nonbiodegradable compounds 22
Novel materials 19

O

Okra mucilage 20
Organic carbon 12
Organic compounds 17
Organic matrix 18
Organic matter 14,20,22,26
Organic pigments 4
Osmosis steps 16
Oxidation methods 13
Oxidation processes 17
Oxidizing agents 20,70,82

P

Peroxicoagulation 18
Peroxidases 29
Petroleum 4
Phosphorus 16
Photooxidation 1
Photocatalytic reactions 21
Photochemical 1,18,71,93,105
Photochemical oxidation processes 18
Photochemical treatment processes 1
Photolytic 17
Photolytic energy 17
Photon source 21
Pilot scale 16
Polarization 16
Polycyclic aromatic hydrocarbons (PAHs) 8
Polysulfone (PS) 16

Polyvinylidene fluoride (PVDF) 20
Potent carcinogens 8
Printing processes 4
Public health concerns 2

R

Reaction chain 17
Real textile wastewater 18
Real wastewaters 1
Reoxygenation 2

S

Scanning electron microscope (SEM) 20
Sedimentation process 15
Sludge flocks 14
Solar radiation 18
Solophenyl Blue (SB) 20
Solophenyl Turquoise (ST) 20
Sonocatalysis 17
Sonocatalysis reactions 17
Sonooxidation 1,2
Sulfonate 20
Surface water sources 3
Suspended solids (SS) 17
Synthetic dye color 29
Synthetic textile 22

T

Textile effluents 22
Textile industry 3,9,13,21,50,61,99
Textile mills 8
Textile product 4
Textile wastewater treatment 1
Textile wastewaters 1
Thermal methods 1,2,22
Total mineralization 14
Transmembrane pressure (TMP) 17
TSS (total suspended solids) 8
Turbidity 20

U

Ultrafiltration 16
Ultrafiltration membranes 16
Ultrasonic cavitation 17
Ultrasonic oxidation processes 17
Ultrasonic treatment processes 1
UV lamps 21

W

Wastewater treatment 1